THE VIEW FROM ROW G

Welsh Writing in English

(General Editors: James A. Davies & Belinda Humfrey)

This volume is published by Seren Books in the above series for the Association for the Study of Welsh Writing in English.

Already published

Caradoc Evans, *My People*, ed. John Harris (1987).
Caradoc Evans, *Nothing to Pay*, ed. John Harris (Carcanet, 1988).
Emyr Humphreys, *A Toy Epic*, ed. M. Wynn Thomas (1989).
Gwyn Thomas, *Three Plays*, ed. Michael Parnell (1990).

In preparation

Idris Davies, *The Longer Poems*.
Glyn Jones, *The Island of Apples*.

DANNIE ABSE

THE VIEW FROM ROW G
THREE PLAYS

Edited by James A. Davies

SEREN BOOKS

SEREN BOOKS is the book imprint of
Poetry Wales Press Ltd
Andmar House, Tondu Road
Bridgend, Mid Glamorgan

The Plays © Dannie Abse, 1990
Introduction and Notes to this editon © James A Davies, 1990

British Library Cataloguing in Publication Data
Abse, Daniel *1923–*
    The view from Row G.
    I. Title
    822.914

    ISBN 1–85411–022–5

*The publisher acknowledges the financial support of the
Welsh Arts Council*

Typeset in 10/12 point Plantin by Megaron, Cardiff
Printed by Dotesios Printers Ltd, Trowbridge

Contents

Acknowledgements

The editor is grateful to Dannie Abse for his help in preparing this edition and to both Dannie and Joan Abse for their friendly hospitality. His thanks also go to Professor R.W. Williams, University College of Swansea, for help with a note on Rilke.

Introduction

Dannie Abse has a distinguished international reputation as a poet. He is well-known as a writer of prose, in particular of the autobiographical novel, *Ash on a Young Man's Sleeve* (1954). Fewer people know that he has had success as a playwright.

His interest in the theatre began in his schooldays in Cardiff. *A Strong Dose of Myself* (1983) has a lively and candid chapter on his early enthusiasms for Bernard Shaw and Eugene O'Neill and his first theatre-going. In a rattling tramcar, *en route* for *Desire Under the Elms* Abse's recklessly confident admiration of O'Neill drew from his friend Sidney Isaacs "a new, inadvertent admiration. Perhaps he felt that I should be one of those fancy, bitch theatre critics who pronounce in the Sunday papers after they have sat, free-ticketed, proud and pampered, in a gangway seat, row G." A few years later he became a less-grand version of that pampered person: when a medical student in London and reviewing off-West-End plays for a small theatre magazine, he was forever, it seemed, taking his "seat in row G among a sparse audience".

This volume could have been entitled *Three Plays* or *Selected Plays*. Its very different title, Abse's own, makes two points. First, these works are *plays*, written for the stage and for an audience. Second, they are aimed, if not directly at a theatre critic, at a thoughtful, critically-minded theatre-goer, whether in row G, the dress circle, or standing at the back. These are serious plays; they are also gripping, moving and often very funny.

That early enthusiasm for the theatre, sustained by visits to Cardiff's Prince of Wales Theatre and the short stint as minor drama critic, made it inevitable that, sooner or later, Abse would try his hand at play-writing. Following the acceptance by Hutchinson of *After Every Green Thing* (1948), his first book of poems, he dramatized part of Balzac's story, *'El Verdugo'* ('The Executioner'), as a poetry-drama called *Fire in Heaven* and offered it to The Questors Theatre in Ealing, the important amateur company often used as a show-case for dramas of ideas.

This, to quote the author, "inept" first attempt became *Is the House Shut?*, produced at The Questors in 1964. Later it was again revised to become *In the Cage*. The theme is the clash between conscience and dreadful orders, in this case to execute one's own family because of the terrorist activities of a single member. As such it is an important precursor of *The Dogs of Pavlov*. Equally important is the continuing link with The Questors Theatre, strengthened through the sequence of revisions and strengthened again in 1962 when *The Joker* and the one-act drama *Gone* were produced there. For apart from its value as a try-out venue The Questors, in John Elsom's words, was a place of "high artistic idealism" that fostered Abse's brand of highminded entertainment.

In 1957, three years after the highly successful *Ash on a Young Man's Sleeve*, Abse published his third volume of poetry, *Tenants of the House: Poems 1951-56*. Included was 'The Meeting', which in 1958 was adapted for the radio in dramatized form. This is a derivative work which has been omitted from *White Coat, Purple Coat: Collected Poems 1948-1988*, Abse's most recent volume of work he wishes to preserve. It is easy to see why: the poem is heavily and prolixly indebted to the Eliot of *Prufrock* and to the social poetry of the 1930s. In a world of problems and broken promises unspecified people move through a 'mean city' to a shabby hall to wait for a 'Speaker' who does not arrive to make real their 'one dream'. From this source came *House of Cowards*, first performed in 1960 to open the Questors' first Festival of New Plays. Directed by John McGrath, it won the 1960 Charles Henry Foyle Award for the best play produced outside the West End and was selected by J.C. Trewin for inclusion in volume 23 of *Plays of the Year*. But, though options were sold, a West End production never materialized and not until 1963 was the play professionally produced. This was, ironically, at Abse's old haunt, Cardiff's Prince of Wales Theatre, where the Welsh Theatre Company, under Warren Jenkins, had its headquarters. The opening coincided with the worst of the hard winter of 1963; in a badly heated theatre that few could reach because of the weather the play died the death.

This was not due wholly to snow and ice. Despite an initial favourable critical response Abse considered that a professional performance had exposed faults, notably the inclination to overstatement in dialogue requiring pruning. A coolly objective view came in 1973, from John Elsom. The Questors' influence, he considered, shows itself in Abse's use of moral allegory, which combines very uneasily with the play's naturalistic detail. In addition the themes are derivative, the stock characters lacking in depth and context.

Despite such criticism *House of Cowards* has refused to go quietly. In 1967 it was published in *Three Questor Plays* and, two years later, found itself, with Aeschylus, Shakespeare, Molière, Ibsen, Brecht, and others of the same rank, in *Twelve Great Plays*, published by Harcourt Brace, the editor, Leonard Dean, having seen *House of Cowards* performed at Ealing. Such recognition is strong evidence of the play's continuing ability to fascinate; it is a strange and compelling piece.

Thus it is no great surprise that almost thirty years after the first performance Abse has returned to the play and revised it extensively to take account of his own and, it would seem, Elsom's main objections. The relationship between the allegorical and the naturalistic has been eased by demystifying the Speaker: he is given a name and a history that includes possible links with charismatic religion. The characters have become more complex and believable: the details of Hicks's dishonest past are made more plausible and his relationship with Doris strengthened; Miss Chantry is changed from a stock spinster in lodgings to an interesting and amusing eccentric who juggles lemons, whistles, has studied comparative religion and occasionally drinks too much; George Hicks's selfish obsession with obtaining a ticket for the Speaker's meeting, out of character in the 1960 version, is now seen in relation to a history of feckless, compulsive gambling; Alf Jenkins, a stage Welshman whose only claim to individuality was his dubious sexuality, emerges as a person of sensibility and some shrewdness. The dialogue is tauter, faster, with fewer static, set speeches and with more accessible contemporary references. The result is still a serious play with a distinct lyrical element, but, now, a tighter one, with the ideas more effectively dramatized.

Through the 1960s Abse's versions of *Fire in Heaven*, as has been noted, kept him preoccupied with the "question of obedience to an evil command". Poems like 'Postmark', 'Not

Beautiful', and the slightly later 'No More Mozart', bear witness to his abiding concern with the Holocaust. Out of such thinking came *The Dogs of Pavlov*, first performed, once again at The Questors Theatre, in the New Plays Festival of 1969. That such a play came when it did in Abse's career is due to two other stimuli. First, as the author acknowledges, was W.H. Auden's essay, 'The Joker in the Pack', which, mainly in relation to Iago, discusses practical joking and deception as evidence of a need for power and as the expression of contempt for others. Second, crucially, was Abse's discovery of an experiment at Yale University devised by Professor Stanley Milgram. Milgram was interested in "the compulsion to do evil" and sought to test the extent to which men "would obey commands that were in strong conflict with their conscience". He advertised for volunteers to take part, they believed, in an experiment to investigate how punishment furthers learning. One 'volunteer' (in reality an actor or actress) was fastened to an electric chair and given verbal tests. If he or she gave wrong answers another volunteer was ordered to administer electric shocks that increased in intensity to a level that caused great pain and threatened life. In reality, the experiment was faked; the volunteers believed they were administering electric shocks whereas their victim was only simulating discomfort and great pain. Milgram discovered that almost all his volunteers — often invoking the interests of science — were willing to reject the dictates of conscience and pull the levers, no matter what might be the observed effect on the victim.

Abse was disturbed by the implications of the experiment, the unethical nature of the deception as well as the responses of the volunteers. As he writes: "[Many] may feel that in order to demonstrate that subjects may behave like so many Eichmanns the experimenter had to act the part, to some extent, of a Himmler." *The Dogs of Pavlov* is a consequence of such feelings; such feelings give the play its great power.

Certainly it was well received at The Questors: after the first performance the theatre was packed and tickets at a premium. Part was televised on BBC 2. The after-performance discussions — a feature of The Questors' festivals — were exceptionally lively explorations of "power and manipulation, racial prejudice and victimization, and even scientific experimentation" using human guinea-pigs. From Gary O'Connor, theatre critic of the

10

Financial Times, came lavish praise: the play was "a work of exceptional merit, well worthy of transfer. A tragedy of feeling . . . if not in actual fact . . . ." It was an exploration of the "criminal (Eichmann) mentality . . . the incipient Nazism in the ordinary man in the street's attitude". The characterization, O'Connor continued, was "hard and objective", the moments of comedy "hilarious".

But the play did not transfer and to date has not received a single professional production in the United Kingdom. It was given an amateur production at Westminster Hospital. There was some continental interest: it was performed in Paris in a French translation, the German rights were sold though no performance resulted. And in 1973 the play was published with an introductory essay by Abse, entitled 'The Experiment', and two letters from Milgram, the first on the essay, the second on the play.

The essay begins by arguing that only the calamities of recent history are real to us and no-one properly understands the 'psychic devastation' of modern atrocities such as the Holocaust and the dropping of the Atomic Bomb. For Abse, as I have already noted, such events raise disturbing questions about human nature: certainly we cannot be convinced that only Germans were capable, say, of persecuting Jews. Indeed, the history of modern Jewish persecution makes only too clear "the willingness of apparently ordinary people to obey evil commands" in Germany and elsewhere. He devotes a short section to the way people are conditioned to obey: "We are trained by punishment and reward, by threat and promise", and then describes Milgram's experiment and its troubling conclusions. Abse makes much of the fact that the volunteers were "hoaxed, fooled", that all, from the electric chair to the victim who was really an actor, to the ostensible aim of the experiment, "was bullshit, a cover story". What Milgram really wanted to know was "how much, to what degree, you would submit to a respectable, apparently reasonable authority — despite the pain and agony of your 'victim' and your slowly awakening conscience".

The last part of the essay is mainly taken up with ethical considerations regarding the conscious motives of the experimenter, the free consent of the subject experimented on,

11

and whether harm was done to the subject, concluding that the Milgram experiment divested the volunteers of all human dignity. But Abse also notes, crucially for our understanding of his dramas, that some of those who pulled the levers were defiant, in great conflict with their consciences, or actively deceived the experimenter by pretending to administer higher doses. He concludes that in this there is cause for at least some optimism.

The essay and then a copy of the play were sent to Milgram who replied, in two letters written early in 1972, that he considered himself perfectly justified in carrying out the experiments. The volunteers were not guinea-pigs but "individuals confronted with a moral choice". One in particular had his life changed through participation: his consciousness of a conflict between orders and personal beliefs led him to refuse the Vietnam draft and become a conscientious objector. Participants were not necessarily victimized, as Abse seemed to think. Some were liberated. In any case, "only the participant knows whether deception had the character of a demeaning experience".

Since then, *The Dogs of Pavlov* has been premiered in the U.S.A. in a performance directed by Maurice Edwards at New York's Cubiculo Theatre. Attempts to arrange a post-performance debate with Milgram came to nothing, as did a proposal to perform the play at Yale.

The Dogs of Pavlov is a powerful and demanding play that requires a professional standard of performance. Abse's revisions — it has been very extensively revised — have made it an even stronger and more demanding dramatic vehicle. The original three-act structure has been reorganized into two Acts, the first ending, with a fine sense of theatre, with Harley-Hoare taking part in the experiment. Further, in the original version the author suggested that film accompanied by music could be shown between scenes, such film to show the relationship between Sally Parsons and John Allison against a lyrical background. This film was to "assist in bleeding off tension". Nowadays sweeping romantic camera-work in, as Abse suggests, London parks, have become clichés of popular advertising and the author is wise to remove it. Tension is now released by a more interesting, semi-dramatic device. Act Two, Scene Two, follows two intensely dramatic scenes: Act One, Scene Five, has Harley-Hoare pulling the levers with Sally as subject; Act Two, Scene One, dramatises

Sally's nightmare. But in Act Two, Scene Two, Doctor Daly lectures on his work, the text of the lecture being, in the main, part of Abse's essay, 'The Experiment'. Not only does this provide the audience with some emotional relief but it also creates, within the play itself, a clear, intellectual context for Daly's experiment.

The revisions, then, clarify central themes. In addition, through extensive pruning and some rewriting of the dialogue both Doctor Daly and Doctor Jones become fuller characters and Sally's romantic vulnerability is pointed up. Most importantly, there is an increase in tension between the doctors and between them and Sally, reflecting the uneasy nature of the scientific enterprise.

The publication of *The Dogs of Pavlov* in 1973 was preceded by that of *Funland and Other Poems*, Abse's sixth volume of poetry. The title poem is a long sequence in nine sections set in an insane asylum. It is a surrealistic work dramatizing the idea of life without central aim or purpose. In 1971 the poem was broadcast on BBC Radio 3 and in introducing it Abse referred to what had become an important theme in his work: "the contemporary white coat of Medicine and the old purple cloak of charismatic Mesmer — their relationship and opposition to each other". This clash between medicine and magic has since been explored in the poem 'Carnal Knowledge' and given prominence as the title of his *Collected Poems 1948-1988*. It is at the heart of *Pythagoras (Smith)*.

Following the broadcast of 'Funland' a dramatized version of the poem-sequence was performed by students of the New College of Speech and Drama. Experiencing this made Abse attempt his own dramatization and for a first performance he turned yet again to The Questors Theatre, who included it in its New Plays Festival of 1975. As Abse admitted, "It was far from being a success". But its potential was recognized by Gary O'Connor, once more in *The Financial Times*, who saw the character of Pythagoras as central to the developing play and suggested that Thomas Mann's short story, 'Mario and the Magician', would indicate dramatic possibilities. "So," wrote Abse in his introduction to the published version of the play,

I took Mr O'Connor's advice: I re-read the Mann story, I re-

13

remembered my own experience as a medical student and as a visitor
to mental hospitals, and keeping in mind Coleridge's dictum that
comedy is the blossom of the nettle, wrote 'Pythagoras'.

The play received its first performance at Birmingham
Repertory Theatre on 22 September 1976. It was well received:
the *Daily Telegraph* reviewer, for example, praised its theatrical
effectiveness and its touching humour; Michael Billington, in the
Guardian, was impressed by "a play that blends intelligence with
delight in theatrical effect". A later review of a performance at the
Gatehouse Theatre Club was also full of praise for the
approachable seriousness and humour of the piece. A broadcast
followed in 1978, also well received, and publication in 1979, in a
volume that included the 'Funland' poem. Reviews of this
volume include that by John Cassidy in *Poetry Review*, citing the
"flexible and expressive dialogue" and the effective theatricality
of the work, plus the "zany humour, high spirits and very good
jokes". Both Alun Rees, in *Poetry Wales*, and Tony Curtis, stress
the increased accessibility of the play compared to the poem.
Since then it has received numerous performances and won a
Welsh Arts Council award.

The text now reprinted is the published version of 1979. The
only change is to the title: the plain *Pythagoras* becomes the
enigmatic *Pythagoras (Smith)*. The absence of revisions reflects
understandable authorial satisfaction: "I've written one very
good play," Abse said in a television interview in 1983, 'I'm very
proud of it — it's called *Pythagoras* . . . . I think that's a pretty
good play."

. . .

Dannie Abse is Welsh, but also Jewish, and this second fact
must be kept in mind when reading or watching these three plays.
For works that feature, respectively, an eagerly awaited Speaker
who will transform unsatisfactory lives, a doctor who tricks
volunteers into taking part in experiments during which,
invariably, the will to obey over-rides conscience, and doctors
who impose strict authority on the strange and nonconformist,
reflect Abse's Jewishness, as has been briefly suggested, through
their disturbing links with aspects of the Holocaust.

In *House of Cowards* the audience is left in no doubt about the connections. Thus, when the Speaker fails to arrive Alf Jenkins, the ambiguous Welshman lodging with the Hickses, still longs for "a new political prophet". George Hicks retorts: "If it's someone like Hitler you're talking about, some demagogue like that, then you're up the pole." "I didn't mean anyone like that," replies Alf, but he protests slightly too much. During the same scene Bill Hicks lights a cigarette and returns us to the Hitler period and its aftermath by remarking: "Immediately after the war in Germany, in 1945, you could get yourself a woman, so they say, wiv one of these." Such references resonate through the play.

The Dogs of Pavlov is permeated with reminders of the worst excesses of the Third Reich. Ironically, Doctor Daly, who is responsible for the experiment to investigate man's capacity for evil, as a medical student worked in the death camps of 1945. The experience was harrowing:

> . . . I can't forget what happened. I can't forget what I saw. I keep thinking how somewhere still, if the register should be called, the answer would come back: "I am Auschwitz, I am Belsen, I am Buchenwald, I am Dachau."

His experiment has convinced him of the capacity for evil of all ordinary people, regardless of race or country. As he says in some of Abse's most affecting lines, later reworked into his poem 'Case History':

> In the course of a single day, after seeing the usual Smiths and Robinsons, have we not listened to the heartbeat of an Eichmann, seen the X-ray of a Hitler, palpated the liver of Goering, read the electroencephalograph of Goebbels?

In the play the links are strengthened by the fact that Kurt is half German, his father dying an unrepentant Nazi, and by Harley-Hoare's revelations of wartime blood-lust.

Such explicit references are absent from *Pythagoras* but its main statement, as Abse wrote of 'Funland', that "the earth . . . is a lunatic asylum whose inmates live out suffering lives of black comedy", plus the play's restating of the 'white coat/purple coat' theme in terms of imposed authority, have all-too-plain Holocaustic relevance.

15

Yet, though Abse is haunted by that most devastating of atrocities, his great strength is his ability to perceive in it an idea of universal and persisting relevance. For all terrible atrocities in the modern period — the Holocaust, for Jew and non-Jew alike, perhaps most of all — are supreme and salutary examples of the destruction of individual identity. Such identity struggles in vain against being subsumed in the popular movements involving elements of mass hysteria that precede so many acts of general destruction (the plays hint at others beside the Holocaust, such as the consequences of Marxism and the American experience in Vietnam). Such acts are directed against those whose difference from an imposed norm, that is, their persisting individualism, causes them to be isolated as enemies and scapegoats. Put plainly, those whose individual identity has been destroyed hate the sight of it in others and react accordingly.

This loss of identity is the main theme of these three plays. In *House of Cowards* it manifests itself in the dramatizing of powerful social norms to which characters feel compelled to relate. One way in which this can be seen is in the characters' obsession with constructing versions of their pasts — for example, Bill Hicks's insistence on the unfairness of his previous employers in dismissing him, and Miss Chantry's tragi-romantic fantasy — as a way, not only of explaining to others the present inadequacies of their lives, but also as a means of continuing to fit in, of being acceptable to a world that values employment and being married. In the same play the use of popular songs makes a similar point — they reflect a *shared* evasive nostalgia — as does Bernard Jay, a journalist on a 1950s tabloid. He is a purveyor of dreams for the masses. It is no accident that he is the publicist for a Speaker, Shemtov, who seeks to bring about, in Jay's words, "transient self-extinction", or, as Miss Chantry puts it, "a temporary annihilation of the self". What this can mean is made only too clear in one of the play's most powerfully theatrical scenes, Act Two, Scene Two, when Nott, who may or may not be the expected Speaker, harangues a crowd desperate for Shemtov's arrival. He tells them that they should not seek to escape from self and present but should "accept even our own terror of ignorance, this here and now, this time, this earth". They should reject the sinister possibilities of what Nott calls — it is one of Abse's most evocative phrases — "the Night's infirmary", the escape into the provided dream. But the latter is what the crowd desires. They grow more menacing and become a chanting, mindless mob. Nott is terrified but to the end clings to his belief in individual responsibility: "When we're all perfect, he will have arrived."

The Dogs of Pavlov is a second exploration of dehumanizing tendencies of which S.J. Gordon is exemplar *par excellence*. As harsh employer and racialist he ruthlessly stereotypes. To him Harley-Hoare is a servile skivvy dominated by money, an impression to which the latter does his best to live up; Kurt, Gordon's ward but also his employee, is expected to obey; women are tarts, and coloured people "niggers". In taking little account of personal feelings he is a model for Doctor Daly. For the latter is equally reluctant to recognize individual worth and shares Gordon's capacity for stereotyping. His failure to remember Sally's name is only a small instance of his indifference to the uniqueness of others. Daly regards all as essentially depraved and demonstrates his contempt by deceiving them. Sally is very like him for, as Kurt tells her, she "distrusts everybody and everything". She loathes the volunteers for they are, to her, all one of a kind and she expects them, as indeed, she expects even her lover, Kurt, to ignore her essential humanity. This is a consequence, we learn, of losing her previous lover, the coloured actor, John Allison. He has become an activist with Black Power, yet another cruelly stereotyping group, and is given one of the play's most chilling lines: there is, he says in a a taped interview, "no time for human affection any more".

Sally's nightmare is the climax of *The Dogs of Pavlov* and resembles the mob-scene in *House of Cowards*. A vicious chorus of characters led by Gordon first subdues the vestiges of Kurt's independent spirit then further subsumes individuality in mass response by shouting racialist slogans as it advances threateningly on the sleeping woman: "Kill the nigger lover. Kill the nigger lover. Trust us."

These are powerful scenes and in *Pythagoras (Smith)* there are more, such as Act One, Scene Five, in which Doctors Aquillus and Green use patients in a demonstration-lecture to students, and the patients' concert in Act Two, Scene Four. The former shows what little regard Doctor Aquillus has for his patients' personal feelings. This has been evident throughout, as when, for

17

example, he wants X to volunteer for the demonstration. He regards X simply as a clinical exhibit and cries for help go unheeded:

X: My bowels are made of glass.
Aquillus: Yes, yes.
X: I feel dead inside.
Aquillus: We'll talk about that later.

There is humour here, of course, but the audience's edgy laughter increases its awareness of Aquillus's exploitative nature. In the lecture itself, his patronizing jokes, his impatient orders, and, in particular, his callous rebuttal of X's claim that he is dead by scratching his arm with a needle, plus his concern to impose psychological theory on all responses, degrade his charges by ignoring them as individuals. This disturbing lack of sympathetic imagination is again evident during the concert. Aquillus is patronizing and manipulative, hardly bothering to distinguish between student, staff and patient, let alone with how they might wish to react: as Arthur prepares to recite Aquillus instructs the asylum audience: "But tonight he has agreed to read us a new poem. Please keep your hands in the applauding position . . . ." The Banchaeri madrigal — a reminder that Abse's sometimes arcane details are invariably significant — in which performers amuse by sounding like animals, indicates to us that the audience within the play views the concert as a chance to be amused by the strange antics of the seemingly sub-human. Significantly the concert becomes another mob-scene (Charlie's rabble-rousing in Act One, Scene Four, being the first) as all, including us, chant nonsense in order to encourage Marian's strip-tease. She has been reduced to sex-object, Pythagoras to amusing charlatan, and we (students, medical staff, audience) discover how easily individuality is lost and human dignity stripped away.

If this was all that could be said these three plays would be unbearably pessimistic. In fact, they are far from being that; Abse's texts, strengthened by revisions, are full of life, humour and individual gestures against imposed authority. All three plays, *Pythagoras (Smith)* in particular, insist on the strange and unique in human nature. All three plays emphasize eccentric, even if, at times, reprehensibly eccentric, behaviour, such as

George's gambling, Bill Hicks's unexpected sexuality, Miss Chantry's interest in jazz, Sally's sloganizing, Kurt's fascination for a green Ming vase, Arthur's singing, Biddy's religious longings, and Pythagoras's belief in his own reincarnation and what seem to be magical powers. The plays hum with life and interest and one repeated detail sums up much. In *House of Cowards* Miss Chantry's ability to juggle is shared with Kurt's father in *The Dogs of Pavlov*. Kurt recalls: "He'd taken three lemons from a bowl on the sideboard . . . and he's juggling them. To amuse me . . . . He appears to be utterly happy . . . . My father's face is uplifted and lit up from within, and he's juggling . . . . I think of him juggling lemons and happy." That the intense moment of happy, carefree, individualistic activity for which almost all Abse's characters strive is dramatized by an activity at once unusual, skilful and absorbing, yet vulnerable and temporary, shows us how greatly eccentricity is prized. We also experience the sadness underlying these lively texts.

In impressive scenes characters protest directly against external controls, as Nott does so powerfully, as Kurt does when Sally tries to test his essential humanity, and as X does against Aquillus's wish to use him as an example for students. But usually characters protest, as it were implicitly and often unconsciously, by demonstrating their unique imaginative potential through the language they use. We are constantly reminded that these are the plays of a fine poet and have their roots in Abse's early attempts to write poetic drama.

A few examples must serve to explain and illustrate. In *House of Cowards* Miss Chantry recalls attending a religious meeting during her youth: "What that voice said, I don't remember. I can only recall understanding everything at the time and feeling inexplicably jubilant, yet peaceful." The intense, poetic, almost tactile cadence of "inexplicably jubilant, yet peaceful", replacing the flatter, colloquial tones of Miss Chantry's normal mode of speech, indicates her empathatic potential and desire for emotional and personal satisfaction so different from any annihilation of self in a violent mob. Again, from Alf Jenkins in the same play: "I'm so looking forward to hearing Mr Shemtov. I've always enjoyed listening to those with the gift of the gab. I like harmonious cadence, even when it's only for vain amusement." The effect is similar: even Alf, very much a man-in-the-street, in a phrase like "harmonious cadence" is moved to aesthetic yearning. Above all, in *House of Cowards*, Nott, roused by the menacing crowd, cries, in a speech already quoted in part: "No more tell me of the rose's waste. I see our eyes move into a different love. I see our heart forget the Night's infirmary . . . . What value is the grave bedecked with flowers?" Through this momentary transcendence of naturalism Nott, despite or perhaps because of his unstable mind – a precursor, this, of a theme in *Pythagoras (Smith)* – emerges as the truly imaginative and therefore compassionate man, grasping instinctively the deathliness of the general longing for a Speaker's panacea.

In *The Dogs of Pavlov* there are similar moments, such as Kurt's description of his father juggling and Sally's reaction to Kurt's news of his New York appointment: "You make New York sound idyllic. It isn't. It's on the road to hell. I doubt if you'll ever see a rainbow in the sky over New York. One day a dove will drown on top of the Empire State Building." Even Daly, perpetrator of the experiment, when telling his colleague of the death-camps, or confronting in his lecture reasons for evil behaviour, abandons the dispassionate stance of the scientist for a language better able to do justice to his dark theme:

> The actual survivors tell their terrible stories of gold from teeth, of lampshades from human skin and so the abstract geography of hell becomes concrete: we see the belching smoke of the chimneys, we hear the hiss of the gas and the dying cries of the murdered. We may not be able to hold steady, in the front of our minds, the enormity of the offence for very long. The picture slips away in the silence between two heartbeats.

In finding such language even Daly reveals a compelling capacity for sympathetic imagining.

From *Pythagoras (Smith)* are three examples. The first is Charlie remembering the past:

> **Charlie**: Coming home excited, looking forward to seeing the wife again, the kids, on a windy autumn afternoon, coming home twenty-four hours early, arms full of things — I dunno — luggage, gifts, flowers . . . .
> **Biddy**: Chrysanthemums . . . .
> **Charlie**: . . . shutting the front door.

Marian: Too loudly.
Ellen: Using one of your feet because your arms are loaded.
Charlie: An' shouting up the stairs, shouting "Hullo, there" . . . .
Nothing. The house empty, the living room empty with a window open.
Marian: That windy autumn afternoon.
Charlie: And the curtains flying, flying.

The second is Arthur's singing, the third Pythagoras's frequent shifts into a non-naturalistic and increasingly exotic mode of speech culminating in his poem, 'White coat and purple coat'.

Pythagoras (Smith), in particular, celebrates the magical, the irrational, the imaginative. Through revealing this last quality, in Abse's work linked closely to the other two, characters remind us of their uniqueness as human beings and are valued for so doing. It is no accident that the two — Nott and Pythagoras — who speak most poetically are the ones who assert themselves most forcibly and hauntingly against conformist and subsuming pressures, and so are the ones with whom the audience most sympathizes. Of course we sympathize with Sally, but in a different way: she is a victim first of circumstances then of the stereotyping self that circumstances have made of her. We sympathize more with Nott, driven out for speaking the truth, and most of all with Pythagoras, reduced to Tony Smith and set for a dreary lifetime in this play's suggested equivalent of a Shelley Street lodging house.

In his supra-naturalistic flights, whether via poetic language or ritualistic structures (for example, the stylized sequence of revelations, retractions and resumptions that closes *House of Cowards*,) Abse is part of the post-war British dramatic movement, led by Beckett, Arden and Pinter, dedicated to making fine theatre from the poetry of ordinary speech. He has been strongly influenced by Pinter: the sexually provocative moments in *House of Cowards* and the interrogation of Kurt during the nightmare scene in *The Dogs of Pavlov*, let alone a recurring atmosphere of menace at times breaking into violence, look back, in particular, to *The Birthday Party*. To make a different kind of link: the close of *House of Cowards*, when characters hurriedly reject the truth about themselves and re-embrace their fantasies, may well reflect the influence of that earlier classic, Ibsen's *The Wild Duck*.

21

But such are the inevitable results of a life-time's interest in the theatre. What must be stressed is that Abse has his own distinctive dramatic voice. These are plays rich in ideas, plays in which he explores not only the Holocaustic ideas already described but also other important themes, such as the relationships between fantasy and reality, work and personal desires, the uses of dreams, the nature of idealism and of trust, aspects of sexuality, the need for religion, and the notion of human life as a constant moral dilemma.

The endings — the need for pretence, the wish to die, the victory of the white coat over the purple — are, in themselves, pessimistic. Nevertheless, to repeat, the plays are not. This is partly because, as it experiences the endings, the audience is on humanity's side, and because the plays as wholes, their action, humour, life and vigour, remind us constantly of the value of that humanity in all its diversity. Further, amidst all that diversity we recognise a common desire for love and grasp, what both Nott and Pythagoras know, that the capacity to love guarantees human worth.

Such reminders, such knowledge, may not seem much when set against the black tide of this century's atrocities. To Abse they are all-important, to be treasured because they are all we have. As he puts it in his essay on *The Dogs of Pavlov*:

> There is the parable of the three wise men who walk past a dead dog. The first utters, "What a terrible sight!"; the second, "what a terrible smell!"; but the third who was the wisest of all, remarked: "What beautiful white teeth has that dead dog!" We must find our consolations where we can.

HOUSE OF COWARDS

Characters

Bill Hicks
Alf Jenkins
Doris Hicks
Miss Betty Chantry
George Hicks
Bernard Jay
Sheila
Mr Nott
Spiv
Crowd

ACT ONE

Scene One

(*The scene is the living room of Number 1 Shelley Street, a corner house. Time, an early March evening, 1958. In the armchair nearest to the anthracite stove on the right sits* Bill Hicks *under a standard lamp.* Hicks, *who is about 60, is playing chess with* Alf Jenkins, *a younger man with a small, red, Welsh mouth. As* Mrs Doris Hicks *enters from a rear door right, a van with a loud-speaker passes by in the street. At first the voice booming through the loudspeaker is distant, but becomes louder and intelligible when* Mrs Hicks *opens the window that lies between the rear door right and the left wall door which leads into the hall. The window overlooks a hedge that partially obscures the street outside.*)

Voice: (*outside*) Four, five, six, seven. At seven o'clock. One, two, three . . .
Hicks: (*without looking up from chessboard*) Close the window.

25

Voice: Four, five, six

Alf: (*joining in*) Seven.

Voice: (*fading*) At Sunshine Hall, tomorrow night. One, two, three, four, etc.

Hicks: (*loud*) The draught, it'll set me off coughing. It's an arctic wind.

Mrs Hicks: (*closing window*) It's going now. Twice that van's been around this evening.

(Hicks *has a fit of coughing.*)

Hicks: (*gasping*) That bloody cold air.

Mrs Hicks: Pity the new daffodils this weather.

Hicks: My chest plays me up and she's worried 'bout bleedin' daffodils. C'mon Alf, move.

Alf: I 'ave to go anyway. The Union Committee, you know.

Mrs Hicks: It's a wonder Miss Chantry hasn't come down because of that van. You'd think the prophet Elijah was coming in a heavenly chariot listening to her. She says it's going to be a great religious meeting.

Alf: It's a political meeting, Mrs Hicks. Where's the *New Statesman*?

Hicks: If you're not going to move, I'm not going to play.

Mrs Hicks: Sheila's mother says this Speaker has extraordinary healing gifts.

Hicks: She's a goner, poor thing.

Mrs Hicks: The whole town's excited. And you saw the news on TV last night? The way they've redecorated Sunshine Hall it's fit for a king.

Hicks: Move or resign, for Chrissake.

Alf: (*rising*) So many people are naive about this meeting. I 'eard a story once about a man who lived on the Blasket Islands — you know, off the coast of South West Ireland.

Hicks: You're resigning, are you?

Alf: (*moving from board*) I'll be late for the committee.

Hicks: Well, just make one more move. I gotcher.

Mrs Hicks: What about the man who lived on the Blasket Islands? I love your stories, Alf.

Alf: He was elderly, see. And he'd never been to the mainland. Then one day he rowed over. And at a bazaar he picks up this mirror, a hand mirror, know what I mean? He'd never encountered a mirror before, ever.

Hicks: It's checkmate in two or three moves.

Mrs Hicks: Never seen a mirror before?

Alf: That's right. So he stares into it amazed. Then he smiles at its reflection and says very gently, still smiling, "Father . . . Father."

Mrs Hicks: (*smiling*) That's a very nice story, Alf.

Alf: He takes back the little mirror to the island, rows back with it in his pocket. And every now and then he pulls it out and has a dekko, each time saying sweetly . . .

Mrs Hicks: Father, Father.

Alf: Right. And when he gets back 'ome he doesn't tell his missus and she, noticing that he's behaving curious, becomes suspicious, see. The way he's keeping his hand in his pocket she knows he's hiding something from her. So one evening, when he's in the fields working, she do go through his jacket and pull out the little hand mirror. Remember, she too has never seen a mirror in her whole life. So she stares into it very surprised. Then she says sneeringly, "Ach, it's only an old woman," and throws it away — ha ha.

Mrs Hicks: That's a good one.

Hicks: Bloody daft if you ask me.

Alf: When you're innocent, Mrs Hicks, you get things wrong like that. More than 'alf the people in this town are pig-ignorant about politics. They don't understand the political significance of this Meeting. Like those two old Blasket Island butties, they're makin' a wrong conclusion. (*beginning to exit*) Gawd, I'm going to be late. (*at door*) Call it a draw.

Hicks: I was murderin' you.

(*Exit Alf.*)

Hicks: I 'ad 'im by the short hairs.

Mrs Hicks: Sheila's mother doesn't think it's political. She thinks after the Meeting she'll walk again. Crikey. When our George and Sheila get married, how'll she manage? Sheila does everything for her. And she can't take in boarders like us.

Hicks: George needs ready cash himself. How an intelligent idiot like him should blow 'alf their savings playing poker beats me. Workin' in that Reference Library, looking up all those facts, enough to turn anyone soft in the 'ead.

Mrs Hicks: Sheila's forgiven him so that's all right.

Hicks: 'Ave you noticed how he's allers coming home these

27

days with big news like how deep Lake Titicaca is in Peru? Or like yesterday. "Dad," 'e said — you weren't in the room — "Dad, did you know how often tortoises die of diphtheria?"

Mrs Hicks: What did you say?

Hicks: I said, I said I didn't know tortoises often die of diphtheria.

Mrs Hicks: Poor tortoises.

Hicks: I don't give a bugger what 'appens to bloody tortoises.

(*Begins to cough.*)

Mrs Hicks: It's time for your medicine. I must say I do think your chest is a little bit better since you gave up smoking.

Hicks: It's money 'im and Sheila need, not knowledge of obscure facts 'bout tortoises.

(*Coughs again.* Mrs Hicks *pours medicine into a spoon.*)

Mrs Hicks: It would be nice to get away for a holiday by the sea. It would do your chest good. (*handing spoon over*) Nice for me not to have to do the cooking for a week. Not to have to make the beds. Careful, don't spill it. Not to have to do all the washing and ironing and scrubbing.

Hicks: Vile taste . . . mashed tortoises.

Mrs Hicks: I hope George and Sheila will be happy.

Hicks: That idea I had about the laundries. I thought of it a long time before Bendix. If it hadn't been for my health I coulda made a packet and seen George and Sheila right.

(Hicks *re-arranges chess pieces.*)

Mrs Hicks: You can start off so confident on the journey. Remember, Bill? You get on the train so cheerfully. It goes off and years later you're still in the train only it's stopped at some derelict sidings an' you're not cheerful any more.

Hicks: Oh, put a sock in it, Doris.

Mrs Hicks: Everything rusts away like, with the days. Still you have to count your blessings, don't you? (*pause*) Oh, I forgot to tell you, Bill. Mrs Verney said a gent had been asking about us.

Hicks: What did he want, a room?

Mrs Hicks: He was a journalist down from London to cover the Meeting. He asked Mrs Verney what family round here took in boarders.

Hicks: He can have Mason's room. Don't let him 'ave it cheap, though.

Mrs Hicks: Then this journalist asks how many in our house and writes down all our names. You, me, George, Alf, Miss Chantry. An' she told him about Mr Mason having a stroke.

Hicks: So?

Mrs Hicks: Then he asked if there was anything special about our house.

Hicks: Special?

Mrs Hicks: Nothing special, she says. It's just Number 1 Shelley Street, a corner house, and then this journalist interrupts and says, "That's great!".

Hicks: What is?

Mrs Hicks: Our house being a corner house. It seemed to inspire him Mrs Verney said . . . .

Hicks: I don't see . . . .

Mrs Hicks: Nor I.

(*Enter* Miss Chantry *from rear door right. She is a rather thin, angular, intense woman over forty.*)

Chantry: Look what I've found. This photo of Harry. Only the top half, I'm afraid, and it's yellowing.

Mrs Hicks: (*taking photo*) Let me put my glasses on . . . .

Hicks: Did you get a ticket for the Meeting, Miss Chantry?

Chantry: No no, but I'll get in.

Mrs Hicks: Oh, he was a handsome fellow. Looks younger than the photo in your room. (*hands it to* Hicks) Looks a bit like Anthony Eden, don't you think, Bill?

Chantry: It doesn't flatter him.

Hicks: All photos flatter us if we wait long enough.

Mrs Hicks: (*smiling*) That's a true word.

Chantry: I wish he were here now — to share with me the experience of the Meeting tomorrow night. Remarkable, isn't it? I mean the Meeting being tomorrow night. Thirty years to the day since poor Harry walked heart-high through the flames into that impossible furnace.

Hicks: Snapshots bring it all back, don't they? (*handing back snapshot*) Oil the old memory, stoke the old fires.

Chantry: He was cremated alive, Mr Hicks.

Hicks: I didn't mean. Sorry. I . . . .

(*Enter* George Hicks, *door left. He is a fresh-faced 22 year old. He carries a number of books and an evening paper.*)

Mrs Hicks: I see you got the books.

George: Yes, they've just come into the Library. *Saturday*

29

Night and Sunday Morning for you, Mum. It's had good reviews. And here's the new Russian novel you asked for, Miss Chantry, *Dr Zhivago*.

Hicks: What about me?

George: For you *Kings of Chess*. (*goes over towards his father*) When I am ze white I win because I am ze white.

Hicks: And when I am ze black I win because I am Botvinnik.

George and **Hicks:** (*together*) Ha!

(*Through the closed window the voice of the loudspeaker van is heard.*)

Voice: (*outside*) Four, five, six, seven. Tomorrow night at Sunshine Hall. At seven o'clock. One, two, three (*fading*) four, five, six etc.

Chantry: It's a miracle, the Speaker coming to our town.

George: Seen the paper? Special Edition all about the Meeting. About the Speaker too, how Adam Shemtov came to be known to everybody simply as the Speaker.

Hicks: What's it say? SPEAKER SHOCK. Ha ha. Have you noticed about headlines, there's always a shock in it? RAILWAY SHOCK, ARSENAL SHOCK, BUDGET SHOCK.

George: Out in the streets today it's like . . . like at the end of the war. On Victory Day. Like that. At the Town Hall the flags are up and the bunting. Everybody seems happy.

Chantry: Naturally.

Hicks: Everybody's gone over the top. Where's our English restraint? Speaker, bloody 'ell. Why don't they call 'im by his real name, Adam Shemtov? I'll tell you why. 'Cause they want to forget he's a foreigner, that's why.

Mrs Hicks: Well, Bill, Adam is a nice English name, isn't it?

(*Pause.*)

Chantry: I doubt if the original Adam spoke English, Mrs Hicks.

Hicks: Eve didn't, ha ha. She was very un-English.

Chantry: How do you mean?

Hicks: It was excess with 'er too. She'd been warned, "Don't eat that apple," right? Picture 'er under the tree with this forbidden apple in 'er 'and, something she'd never tasted before, a mystery fruit, bringin' it up to her mouth, sniffing it, letting it touch her lips lightly, half expectin' it to explode or somethin'. Then, seeing nothing 'appened, she took a little bite.

Then waited to see what disaster would strike. Nothin'. The birds of Paradise continued to sing, the butterflies staggered around, the bees buzzed. Nothing changed. So she took another bite, and then another bite, munch munch munch, till she'd finished off the bleedin' lot. That done for 'er. She'd gone over the top. If she'd stopped at that first little nibble, when the devil's hand was only half way up her thigh, she would 'ave been all right. But she had no restraint, no English restraint.

Chantry: That's a very interesting way of considering the *Book of Genesis*, Mr Hicks.

Hicks: You're all over the top. The whole town's over the top. This meeting, I'm telling you is a load of rose-crap, this foreign speaker a phoney.

Chantry: No, no.

George: You assume any public speaker is a phoney, every promise insincere.

Chantry: Every programme uncertain or tepid or cynical or dishonest.

George: The Speaker coming here, to our town now, March 1958, why that's something momentous, strange.

Hicks: Rubbish.

Mrs Hicks: Don't you understand, Bill? I think I understand.

Chantry: Once I saw something quite perfectly, I understood the pattern of all things in their entirety.

Hicks: Oh no! For Gawd's sake!

Chantry: It happened once. I was 22, about your age, George. It was like hearing a great voice. One single whispering voice. What that voice said, I don't remember. I can only recall understanding everything at the time and feeling inexplicably jubilant, yet peaceful. I sometimes wonder whether I heard that voice at all. Maybe it was just my imagination or maybe it was only a silly, pretty dream.

Mrs Hicks: No, no.

Chantry: I have to hear that voice again. I want to be happy like that again in a way I cannot understand or communicate. That's why I'm looking forward to the Meeting. There'll be a great religious revival.

George: It's not religious, Miss Chantry. Nothing to do with religion, not as you mean it anyway.

Mrs Hicks: Alf says its political.

Hicks: Alf thinks everything's political, even football. If he had a girl-friend he'd get over this politics lark. He'd outgrow it.

George: It's not political either. At least not in the way Alf thinks it is.

Hicks: Then what is it?

(*Pause.*)

Hicks: He doesn't know. He's talking about it as if it's all strawberries and cream but he hasn't a clue.

Chantry: Haven't you ever been moved by singing a hymn, Mr Hicks?

George: It's difficult to define. If I say it's moral you'll . . . .

Hicks: Moral? Ha ha.

George: We're all sick with avarice. There's a war going on in Algeria. There's the Bomb. You don't understand. They say he's the greatest orator ever. We're all asleep and men asleep are men enslaved. He'll awaken us all to a full consciousness of what we are.

Hicks: Ho. That would be a disaster, that would. Ho.

Mrs Hicks: Why are you always pulling things down?

Hicks: (*annoyed*) Morals, he's talking about morals. Didn't he play poker behind Sheila's back? He should talk about morals.

George: When it comes to morals you've got no . . . . Look, do you want me to remind you of one or two things? Your last job . . . .

Hicks: (*quickly*) He needs a haircut. When did you last have a haircut? Not since you finished your National Service I shouldn't think.

George: I must be going, Ma. I'm eating at Sheila's tonight.

Mrs Hicks: But you were out last night. Where were you last night?

Hicks: You look like a spiv with your hair that long.

Chantry: I like your hairstyle, George.

Hicks: Looking like that he'll never get promoted. Junior Librarian! That doesn't put much melon in the fridge.

(Mrs Hicks *goes over to* George, *gently takes him by the arm.*)

Mrs Hicks: You see you eat properly tonight, son.

Hicks: (*to* Miss Chantry) If he went for an interview with his hair that long even Robinson Crusoe wouldn't employ him. Don't turn your back on me. I'm talking to you. You believe in the powers of oratory. Well, I'll tell you. It's only Money that talks.

George: You gave me plenty of that. You gave me a great start. If you weren't so damn lazy, sitting on your arse and — aw hell.

(*Exit* George, *door left.*)

Hicks: (*shouting after him*) Don't speak to me like that.

Chantry: You upset him, Mr Hicks.

Hicks: He should get one of those new crew-cut haircuts like Laurence Harvey in *Room at the Top*.

(*Sound of Front Door being slammed very hard.*)

Hicks: Funny, isn't it — the younger they are, the louder they slam the door. You can tell the age of people just by how loudly they slam front doors.

Mrs Hicks: If Sheila's forgiven him about losing that money there's no need for you to go on about it.

Hicks: Sheila wanted to save all that dough for setting up house, that was sensible.

Chantry: Supposing he doesn't turn up?

Hicks: If I had money myself I'd give it 'im.

Chantry: Supposing the Speaker doesn't turn up?

Mrs Hicks: Of course he'll turn up. It's been so widely advertised.

Hicks: Miss Chantry, if I had my health, a decent pair of lungs, I wouldn't have packed in that last chauffeuring job and I would have seen him and Sheila right.

Mrs Hicks: They wouldn't have redecorated the Hall if he wasn't going to turn up.

Hicks: I'm talking about important matters and you're blabbering on about this bleedin' Meeting.

Chantry: You don't understand, Mr Hicks, you don't understand anything.

Hicks: Since I don't understand, since I'm so ignorant let me ask you a question.

Mrs Hicks: (*warningly*) Bill!

Hicks: Who put up the advertisements?

Chantry: For the Meeting?

Hicks: Yes, go on. Tell me that, go on.

Chantry: I don't know.

Hicks: Whose van was that going round with the megaphones?

Chantry: I don't see.

Hicks: You don't see. You mean you don't know. Who hired the hall for this Adam Whatsisname?

Chantry: I never thought.

Hicks: Isn't it time you thought?

Chantry: (*defeated*) I don't know. (*pause*) You're destructive. Your husband is a bully and very destructive.

Mrs Hicks: Now don't get upset, dear.

Hicks: Destructive? I'm destroyed. Without health one's destroyed.

Chantry: You shouldn't be so sorry for yourself. You've got a son, a good boy, a pleasant boy. Fire robbed me of my children.

(*Hurried exit, door right.*)

Hicks: (*calling after her*) It's all cooked up, that Meeting. (*quietly to* Mrs Hicks) For fools like her and George and Alf.

Mrs Hicks: You're getting worse. You're getting impossible with everybody.

Hicks: She gets on my wick. She and her hero, Harry Wallace. That photo. Caw.

Mrs Hicks: You should be more considerate. Miss Chantry's very thin-skinned.

Hicks: She's very spiritual, I'll give you that. If you held her up to the light you'd see her soul.

Mrs Hicks: We'll lose her as a tenant the way you behave. And you really hurt George. Somebody's got to stand up to you. One can only take so —

Hicks: Aw, come on, love. I don't feel so great. I'm sorry if I went over the top with George. Look, I wheezed so much last night I hardly had any sleep.

Mrs Hicks: You slept like a log. It was me who was awake. (*pause*) I kept thinking of the old days. How it used to be with us.

Hicks: It's still all right with us. Isn't it all right with us, Doris?

(*Pause.*)

Look, love (*sincerely*) I couldn't live without you. I love . . . I mean.

Mrs Hicks: Yes, I know. I know.

Hicks: I had a strange vivid dream last night. I dreamt you were flirting like mad with a black-gowned Roman Catholic priest.

Mrs Hicks: Me?

Hicks: Yes, you. (*aggressively*) Bloody leading him on, you were. I rugby tackled 'im, as a matter of fact. I took off his shoe and beat the 'ell out of him. (*loud*) You were leading him on, definitely.

(*The front doorbell rings.* Mrs Hicks *is about to answer it but then the telephone also rings.*)

Hicks: Why is it the front door bell and the telephone always ring at the same time?

Mrs Hicks: (*picking up phone*) Hello. Who? Mr Mason. No, I'm sorry Mr Mason passed away. No, no, he's dead. He died a few weeks ago. Hello.

(*Front door bell rings again.*)

Just a minute please. (*holds hand over phone*) Answer the front door, Bill.

Hicks: The draught from the front door starts me off coughing.

Mrs Hicks: Hello, hello. Oh, they've rung off.

Hicks: Better answer the front door then.

Mrs Hicks: Somebody asking for Mr Mason but the line wasn't very clear.

Hicks: Who'd be asking for Mason.

(Mrs Hicks *exits door left to answer front door.* Hicks *begins to whistle 'I can't give you anything but love, baby'. Then abruptly stops. Takes out a cigarette from his pocket. Lights it up. Takes two long puffs before putting it out. Resumes whistling 'I can't give you anything but love, baby'.* Mrs Hicks *and* Mr Jay *enter. The latter is carrying a brand new suitcase.*)

Hicks: What?

Mrs Hicks: This is Mr Jay.

Hicks: He wants a room?

(Jay *puts case down and goes over to shake hands with* Mr Hicks.)

Jay: Bernard Jay of *The Daily Star*. Pleased to meet you.

Mrs Hicks: We take *The Daily Star*.

Jay: I must say you all must be very excited about it. Fantastic.

Mrs Hicks: I've seen your name in the paper.

Jay: There's a feature by me today on 'Dancing in Britain'.

Hicks: Excited about what?

Jay: About the Speaker coming here.

Hicks: Oh, that.

Jay: Sorry to burst in on you like this, Mr Hicks. I hope it's a convenient time?

Hicks: Mason's room is a very good room. Best in the house, I'd say.

Mrs Hicks: I read that article. Fancy, five million a week go dancing in Britain.

Jay: Yes, for a few bob people enter a different world. Lush thick carpets, gilt mirrors, ladies' powder rooms in pastel pinks and blues. All those pretty lights and revolving bandstands make them forget the drabness of their working lives. But the Speaker coming here, that's a bit more than Victor Sylvester, right Mr Hicks?

Hicks: How long do you want the room for, Mr Jay?

Jay: We're going to take pictures of you all. Everybody in this fortunate house. It'll be on the front page. How do you feel about it? I mean about the Speaker staying here.

Hicks: What do you mean here?

Jay: In your house, Mr Hicks.

Mrs Hicks: *Our* 'ouse?

Jay: But as you've probably read, Mr Adam Shapur, the Speaker, never puts up in an hotel. He always stays with a humble family.

Hicks: We're not that humble, ha ha.

Mrs Hicks: Shapur? I thought it was Shemtov? Adam Shemtov.

Jay: I have reason to believe that Shemtov is only a code name. And he is half Persian, you know. There was a King Shapur in the third century in Persia — a Parthian actually, and he granted religious freedom to everybody.

Mrs Hicks: A good man then?

Jay: Well, he hated the Romans. When he captured the Emperor Valerian at the Battle of Edessa he used him first as a footstool, then he had the Emperor flayed alive before getting him stuffed with dung and hung in a temple.

    (*Pause.*)

Hicks: I assume you have some form of identification on you, Mr Jay? A press card or something?

Jay: Oh yes, of course. Here you are. Mrs Hicks, I hope you'll be good enough to prepare his room. You'll be . . . rewarded, of course.

36

Mrs Hicks: Mason's room, Bill?

Hicks: What are you talking about? A bigwig like 'im, whatever his bloody name is, even if he doesn't stay in hotels, wouldn't be staying here — any more than Bertrand Russell would, or Colonel Nasser or Archbishop Makarios.

Jay: I hope you won't mind our presumption but *The Daily Star* sent him a telegram saying you expect him. Your place is only five minutes from both the station and Sunshine Hall. And it's a corner house. You're very lucky.

(Jay *takes cigarettes from his pocket and offers one to* Bill Hicks.)

Hicks: Thank you, no. I've given that habit up.

(Jay *lights cigarette.*)

Mrs Hicks: We are very well situated. The shops are just around the corner in the main road. And we have hot water all the time. Our new Ideal boiler is a boon.

Hicks: Just a mo, Doris. We're not selling the house. True, we are five minutes from Sunshine Hall but so are all the other houses in Shelley Street.

Mrs Hicks: It would be a great honour having the Speaker to stay here. We'd treat him as one of our own.

Hicks: Nobody would stand for that. You 'ave to be blood of our blood to put up with that sort of treatment.

Mrs Hicks: He said we'd be rewarded, Bill.

Jay: *The Daily Star* will run a feature. The Speaker stayed in Number 1 Shelley Street. I'd write it, of course, but in your name.

Hicks: You mean ghost it? Like they do for star footballers?

Jay: Right.

Hicks: Now somebody like Nat Lofthouse or Billy Wright or Johnny Haynes, they'd get a four figure fee, wouldn't they?

Jay: So will you, Mr Hicks.

Hicks: You're kidding!

Jay: You'll be pleased with the article. It'll be a dignified piece — like today's article on 'Dancing in Britain'. Only of course it'll be on the front page. Did you see my piece on the by-election at Rochdale, Mrs Hicks?

Mrs Hicks: I liked the look of the Liberal candidate there. Ludovic something or other. The fellow that married little red shoes, Moira Shearer, Bill.

Hicks: What's the catch, Mr Jay? C'mon, there's a catch, isn't there?

Jay: You're very sceptical. No catch. You'll get a four figure fee. Here's the contract. You keep one and sign the other. Course it's null and void if he doesn't stay here. You'll see that in Clause 3. Just sign there — where I've put the crosses.

Mrs Hicks: Just because we're five minutes from . . .

Jay: Not many around here have lodgers like you do. The fact is Mr Mason's stroke was a lucky stroke for you.

Mrs Hicks: Mr Mason has passed on.

Jay: No disrespect, Mrs Hicks. But I know all about that and that's one reason . . .

Hicks: What do you mean, Mr Jay?

Jay: Look, sometimes something in life happens that's totally unexpected. Something fantastic happens. The iron bar is bent and nothing is quite the same ever again. The Speaker coming here will be like that for you. That's what I'm going to write about.

Mrs Hicks: Sign it, Bill.

Hicks: I want to believe you, Mr Jay.

Jay: Wanting, that's half the battle. You've got nothing to lose. In the most unlikely event of the Speaker staying elsewhere — which he won't — *The Daily Star* would see you right. I'll personally see to it you'll get twenty quid. OK? But it'll be the four figure fee, Mr Hicks, don't you worry.

(Hicks *nods and signs. Hands back the contract.*)

Thank you. By the way, may I leave this case here? I bought it in a shop near the station. A real bargain. I'll pick it up tomorrow when the photographers come.

Mrs Hicks: That phone call. The man who asked for Mason, Bill. Do you think it could have been the Speaker's secretary?

Jay: Phone call? I didn't know about that. Still that's good, ha ha. Very good. (*beginning to exit*) Everything's going to work beautifully.

Mrs Hicks: Tell me, Mr Jay. Is the Meeting a religious one or a political one?

Jay: I . . . er . . . I have a theory — but it's only a theory.

Hicks: Theory?

Jay: I think he'll begin by asking everyone in Sunshine Hall to write down their name and their mother's name on a piece of paper. Then he'll invite them to tear that paper into small fragments. It'll be a symbolic act of transient self-extinction, do you see? By the end of the Meeting all will feel renewed and each have a fresh sense of mission.

Hicks: Is that the sort of thing I'll be writing?

Jay: It's just a hunch.

Hicks: Sounds bonkers. Lotta hogwash.

Jay: Ah well, I must be off. Don't look so worried, Mrs Hicks.

Mrs Hicks: Mason's room, it's nothing fancy, Mr Jay. It's got a washbasin but it, frankly, could do with some re-decorating.

Jay: You don't have to worry about that. You are worried? Look, at the end of the war I was out in Karachi. That's where I first heard of Adam Shapur. They spoke of this remarkable young guru who led an archaeological expedition into the vast salt desert of North Persia. It's one of the most desolate regions in the world and he was out there for God knows how long. If it is the same Adam Shapur that I think it is then he'll find running water in a basin absolute luxury.

Hicks: What was the point of him going out there?

Jay: Near an oasis, overwhelmed thousands of years ago by salt and sandstorms, they discovered some cuneiform tablets. They've never cracked the code, they've never been interpreted and no-one knows where they are. I wrote a feature about it once. The Lost Tablets of Dashti-i-Lut. It's a total mystery. Anyway, since then Adam Shapur has spent other long periods in difficult terrain. He's not someone who expects silk sheets, Mrs Hicks.

Hicks: If he comes here, when do you think he'll come?

Jay: He's due to speak at seven tomorrow evening. There's a train due in from London at 5.35 so I suppose he'll come straight here.

Mrs Hicks: What shall I call him? Do I call him Mr Shemtov or Mr Shapur?

Jay: That's one question you must ask him. All right? See you tomorrow then.

Mrs Hicks: Thank you, Mr Jay. Sometimes in this house we forget to say thank you, don't we, Bill?

Hicks: *(calling)* Mr Jay, you've left the Speaker's case.

Jay: *(at door left)* The Speaker's case? My case, Mr Hicks. Oh! Yes. I see. That case . . . . What an idea! Splendid! He sent it

39

on. Remember that. We'll get a good article out of this, you and me.

(*Exit* Jay.)

Hicks: I don't care what his bloody name is. What his alias is. He's got to stay here. With that money — as the man said — the iron bar would be bent.

Mrs Hicks: I must tell the good news to Miss Chantry. She'll be so excited. (*at rear door right she hesitates*) Should I tell her, Bill?

Hicks: Why not? You can't discount what people say just because of the way they say it.

Mrs Hicks: That's a true word.

Hicks: What I could do with that dough. You say his articles, Bernard Jay's articles, are good?

Mrs Hicks: The one today's very good. The new craze for Rock and Roll dancing. Very good.

Hicks: It must be true. What the 'ell's in it for 'im if it isn't? Just think, Doris. I could give some of the money to George when he gets married. And with the rest I could buy a little car. Oh, not a Sunbeam Rapier with overdrive 'cause that costs over a thousand. That would be too expensive. But a little Morris Minor, say, which isn't too 'eavy on petrol.

Mrs Hicks: A car? That would be extravagant.

Hicks: With a car, love, I could do a job of work again. I'm fed up of sitting on my backside, day in, day out. George bringing his money home and you collecting the rent. It's degrading, not working. With a car I could start a private taxi service from the station. You always say they need more taxis waiting at the station.

Mrs Hicks: It's years since you had that job as a chauffeur.

Hicks: Exactly. What am I living for? This is a chance. The Speaker, why he's my chance to start again.

Mrs Hicks: It would be like a dream come true.

Hicks: My bad chest wouldn't stop me from driving. A car with a good heater.

Mrs Hicks: You know this town like the back of your hand.

Hicks: I'd learn when every train comes into the station. I'd go back to work again. (*stands up*) I'm going to work again. What's the matter, Doris?

Mrs Hicks: But suppose that journalist was just having us on

— for a story. Do you think that's possible?

Hicks: I don't want to hear.

Mrs Hicks: It's a bit unlikely, don't you think, Bill?

Hicks: (*nods his head back and forth as if overcome*) You . . . doubt me? What are you trying to do? Destroy me?

Mrs Hicks: I don't doubt you, Bill.

Hicks: Are we five minutes from Sunshine Hall?

Mrs Hicks: So what?

Hicks: Five minutes from the station?

Mrs Hicks: Yes, but . . .

Hicks: This is a corner house and Mason is dead.

Mrs Hicks: Yes, that's true.

Hicks: And he said *The Daily Star* sent a telegram.

Mrs Hicks: Yes, yes.

Hicks: The Speaker will come here. You had a phone call.

Mrs Hicks: I had a phone call.

Hicks: And didn't Mr Shapur, or whatever his name is, send his luggage on?

Mrs Hicks: That case?

Hicks: Yes, that case.

Mrs Hicks: You said it was the Speaker's.

Hicks: The journalist said it was the Speaker's.

Mrs Hicks: You did, didn't you?

Hicks: No.

Mrs Hicks: Oh.

Hicks: You don't believe me. Then open it. Open the case.

Mrs Hicks: No.

Hicks: (*shouting*) He said it was the Speaker's case. Open it.

Mrs Hicks: It's not ours, Bill.

Hicks: Open it, I say. You'll find proof in there.

Mrs Hicks: We won't bother. I'll just tell Miss Chantry the good news.

Hicks: Bring it HERE.

Mrs Hicks: It's better not to know.

Hicks: (*advances*) Let . . . me . . . have . . . that . . . case.

Mrs Hicks: No, Bill.

(Hicks *grabs the case. He is about to open it but* Mrs Hicks *struggles to keep it closed.*)

Mrs Hicks: It doesn't matter what's inside. Listen to me. That call was from the Speaker's secretary. He said,"There'll be

41

room in Number 1 now Mr Mason's dead."

(Hicks *forces case open.*)

Hicks: Why, there's nothing in it.

Mrs Hicks: That doesn't matter. He'll still be coming here.

Hicks: It's empty.

Mrs Hicks: Are there any marks in it suggesting it belongs to anyone else but the Speaker?

Hicks: No, no, that's so.

Mrs Hicks: (*joyously*) Oh, think what we could do with all that money.

Hicks: Sure.

Mrs Hicks: I'll prepare his room at once.

Hicks: Why shouldn't he send an empty case? A man like that, betcher, has many quirks.

Mrs Hicks: Great men are not like the rest of us, Bill.

Hicks: I'll go to work again.

Mrs Hicks: That's right.

Hicks: I will go to work again, it'll be like old times.

Mrs Hicks: (*at door right and opening it*) Miss Chantry, Miss Chantry.

Hicks: That's it. Tell 'er the good news.

Mrs Hicks: (*calling*) Miss Chantry. Do come down.

Hicks: We'll have a drink to celebrate. We'll have a party.

Mrs Hicks: I do wish she'd hurry. We'll tell Alf too, when he's back.

(Hicks *at sideboard is taking out a bottle and three glasses.*)

Hicks: Everybody. We'll let everybody know. Some people are miserly with good news. Not me. Not the Hicks. You know that joke about the businessman who says to his friend, "You never ask me about business." So his friend says, "How's business?" And the businessman replies, "Don't ask." Ha ha ha.

(*He takes a drink himself and hands one to* Mrs Hicks.)

Mrs Hicks: Ha ha, that's a good one. We'll have everything proper when he comes. Daffs in his room. I could just clap hands.

Hicks: Clap hands, sweetheart. Stamp your feet. The Hickses are back again.

Mrs Hicks: Here's to us, Bill.

(Miss Chantry *enters.*)

Hicks: Ah, my dear, just in time for a little bit of what you fancy.

Chantry: What's . . .

Mrs Hicks: I'm so excited. (*taking her a glass*) Here. I'll tell you about it later.

Hicks: (*raising glass*) To the Speaker.

Mrs Hicks: To the Speaker, God bless him.

Chantry: To the Speaker?

Hicks: I feel like . . . I feel like singing.

Chantry: Perhaps it's because the Speaker's coming.

Hicks: He is coming.

Mrs Hicks: He's coming here.

Chantry: (*triumphantly*) You've seen the truth at last, Mr Hicks. You're not alone any more.

Hicks: Ho no no no no, not you. We're all fond of you here, Miss Chantry, Betty Chantry. I know sometimes I get bad-tempered, speak rough — because I don't feel good. But make no mistake about it, I respect you so . . . drink up.

Chantry: His coming has affected even you. You'll learn nothing is so evil that it's unworthy of love.

Hicks: (*sings*) I can't give you anything but love, baby. C'mon, Doris, you used to like that song. Sing it, Doris.

Mrs Hicks: For Heaven's sake, Bill.

Hicks: (*sings again*) I can't give you anything but love, baby.

Mrs Hicks: (*joining in*) That's the only thing I've plenty of, baby.

(Hicks *takes* Chantry *by the hand and heavily dances with her as* Mrs Hicks *sings.*)

Dream a while, scheme a while, you're sure to find,
Happiness and I guess all those things you've hoped and pined for . . .

Hicks: Sing faster, Doris, faster, faster.

(Mrs Hicks *now sings faster and* Miss Chantry *too is laughing.* Hicks *and* Miss Chantry *dance faster.*)

Chantry: Oh! Oh!

Mrs Hicks: Gee, I'd like to see you looking swell, Betty. Diamond bracelets Woolworth's couldn't sell, Betty. But until that lucky day you know darned well, Betty . . .

All together: I can't give you anything but love. Ha ha ha.

Hicks: Three cheers. Hurrah, hurrah . . .

Hicks and Mrs Hicks: Hurrah.

Chantry: Oh, Mr Hicks, you are really . . .

Hicks: Funny, I'm not out of breath at all. I'm like I used to be when I was young an' could lift hundredweights. I feel strong again. I can't tell you 'ow I feel.

(*Going over to* Mrs Hicks *who still has a glass in her hand.*) 'Ere, give me a kiss, darling.

(Hicks *embraces her forcefully and sexually, right hand on her left breast, and gives her a passionate kiss. For a moment* Miss Chantry *looks disturbed till* Mrs Hicks *pushes her husband away.*)

Mrs Hicks: Ha ha ha. Get away with you, don't be soppy in front of . . . You'd think it was us, not Sheila and George getting married!

(Hicks *takes glass from her hand and deliberately, carefully, places it on the floor, then with his heel crushes it.*)

Chantry: Ooooh!

Mrs Hicks: Ha ha ha.

Hicks: Ha ha ha.

All together: Ha ha ha, ha ha ha.

(*As they laugh lights come down for the end of the Act.*)

ACT TWO

Scene One

(*Time, later that Thursday evening. Scene, a railway bridge not far from Shelley Street. The bridge is on the hump of a hill. The streets beyond, which lead to Sunshine Hall, are out of sight. In the rear, though, the top of a gasholder can be seen distantly. The upper parts of other structures, e.g. derelict-looking warehouses, chimney stacks, etc., also loom up darkly from behind. In front the street curves from the left to the humped bridge and to the right is a lit lamppost which has a loudspeaker attached to it. Because the bridge is slanted from left to right, the left parapet of the bridge is clearly visible over which the characters on stage can peer to the railway lines that lie invisibly below and the other side of it.*

As lights come up a newsboy is shouting distantly off stage.)

Voice: (*off*) Evening Echo. Special Edit-ion. News of the Meeting. Special Edit-ion. New developments. Read all about it.
(George *and* Sheila *enter from left.* George *is reading a newspaper.*)
George: Same as in the earlier edition. 'Cept Sir Harold Tanner is going to be chairman. Funny, Dad worked for him once as a chauffeur.
Sheila: Look, George. On the lamp-post there.
George: They're putting up those loudspeakers on every lamp-post from here to Sunshine Square. The streets will be packed all the way up to this bridge.
Sheila: Don't expect many'll be here though. When the trains go under you'd hardly hear anything.
George: As mother would say — "A true word".
Sheila: I admire your mother. Quietly she's really a strong woman.
George: Behind every strong woman is a weak man!
Sheila: (*going over to parapet*) You're too contemptuous of your

45

father, George.

George: He's so focused on his chest. He keeps looking at the spit he brings up like some people look at their own faeces. An' mother's more like his slave than his wife.

Sheila: She just loves him, George.

(George *joins her. There is a distant sound of a train shunting, trucks clattering, a sad engine whistle,* George *puts his arm round* Sheila.)

Sheila: Isn't it pretty, the lights and signals and things? Which look bigger — those amber oblongs in the windows down there or the stars up there?

George: The night's kind. I mean all the ugliness is gone. See the moonlight glinting on the railway lines? (*pause*) I'd like to do something important one day.

Sheila: Like marrying me.

George: Yeh, like marrying you. (*pause*) Hearing the Speaker together — that's goin' to be important. I got a feeling, maybe it's crazy, but I got a feeling that hearing him will, somehow, change our lives, know what I mean? We'll remember it all our lives. Hearing him together. It'll be something very pure, clean, like snow before anybody walks on it.

Sheila: Let's come here tomorrow night. Hear him on this bridge together.

George: You know the price of the tickets on the black market is impossible. Well, last night I er — don't go up in the air, Sheila, but . . . .

Sheila: But what? C'mon, don't start something an' not finish it. I hate that.

(George *takes envelope out of his pocket.*)

George: £43.15 shillings. I won it last night at the Clubhouse. I could buy two tickets with this.

(Sheila *breaks away from him.*)

Sheila: God, you're trouble. You're really trouble.

George: I won.

Sheila: That's not the point.

George: I couldn't help having four aces! Fate dealt me four aces, kid.

Sheila: You promised.

George: You take the money then. Put it in our savings.

(*He offers her the envelope. She does not take it.* Mr Nott

46

enters right from furthest side of the bridge, unobserved by George *and* Sheila.)
Don't grump, Sheila, I . . .
Nott: Excuse me. So sorry. Just want to know if the London express has passed under the bridge yet? The train's due, I think.
George: It hasn't passed while we've been here.
(Mr Nott *goes over to the bridge and makes as if to climb on to the parapet.*)
Sheila: George!
(George *rushes to stop him.*)
George: You can't do that. For heaven's sake.
Sheila: Stop him, stop him.
Nott: (*giving up*) I can't. I'd have to climb up on that parapet. I'd watch the train come, then I'd have to jump before that bellowing iron engine. Brr. In theory, simple. But in practice? (*with back to them, looking over bridge*) It would be nothing, that's all. (*swivels round to face them and almost shouts*) Nothing, do you understand? No, that's impossible to understand.
George: You're not going to wait for that train?
Nott: I don't know. I can imagine my own shriek the second before death, my limbs crunching under the iron monster, the noise a backbone makes when broken in half . . .
(Sheila *and* George *look at each other.*)
George: Who are you? I mean who . . .
Nott: I used to think I was John Neil or Frank Dixon or Roy Morley.
Sheila: Who are they?
Nott: Yes, naturally you're puzzled. It's unusual. Most deluded people imagine themselves to be much more grandiose. Some of my late colleagues imagined they were King Henry the Eighth or the Duke of Wellington or Lord Nelson — depending on what used to be their local pub, I suppose!
(*He laughs, but* George *and* Sheila *just stare at him uneasily.*)
I was making a joke and it was in bad taste. Excuse me.
Sheila: Then you're from a mental hospital?
Nott: I was, yes.
Sheila: You escaped?
Nott: No no no. I've been discharged. They purged me of every bizarre dream. My name is Nott. Nott like my father and his father before him. You're still puzzled. Of course, I haven't

explained. I used to think I was Mr Morley or Mr Neil or Mr Dixon. Ordinary people. Nothing special. I just wanted to be anyone but myself — that's how they explained it to me. Wanting to be someone else is half the trouble. When you believe yourself to be another person, however commonplace, that puts the lid on it. Psychotic delusions, yes. Still with shocks, I became myself again. Plain Mr Nott.

George: You're not from this town, are you?

Nott: I couldn't go back to Reading. Once you've been in for treatment your old neighbours regard you with suspicion. It's worse than being a criminal. It doesn't matter how sane you are, they expect you to do funny things.

George: Like jumping off bridges?

Nott: I had a nice little business in Reading. Never mind. I thought it best to take a bit of a holiday before starting somewhere new and I happen to have a friend in this town. I can see you're still worried, Miss. I'm all right now.

Sheila: All right now? Then why do you want to throw yourself off the bridge?

Nott: I explained to you. I have no dreams left. They took them away from me one by one and now there's nothing left. Nothing. No, no, that's a lie. I wouldn't throw myself down there. I haven't the courage anyway.

George: Did you say you've a friend here?

Nott: Chap by the name of Mason. I used to be friends with him years ago. Sent me a Christmas card every year. But now I've arrived I don't want to see him particularly. I did phone him but I think I got the wrong number. Anyway, it doesn't matter. There's plenty of time.

Sheila: He doesn't mean that Mr Mason who lived in your house?

George: It's a common enough name. There's something fishy about his story.

Nott: I beg your pardon?

Goerge: Where are you staying, Mr Nott?

Nott: I've got a room at the Imperial tonight. Tomorrow I don't know where because everywhere seems fully booked.

George: You didn't come here because of the Meeting tomorrow night? That's why the hotels are so full.

Nott: The Meeting? Oh no. Lots of people seem to be talking about the Meeting. Yes, and about this charismatic Mr Shemtov. At the hospital I asked Dr Daybrook why so many people these days had reported seeing unidentified flying objects visiting our planet from outer space. He told me that in this thermonuclear age people are so anxious about their imminent destruction, so aware that they can't control their own fate, that they are longing for superior beings to save them from their own mischievousness.

Sheila: So?

Nott: Oh. I was just thinking. Could it be like that with this Mr Shemtov?

George: Well, shouldn't we move on, Sheila?

Sheila: Where are you going Mr . . . er?

Nott: Not Mr Dixon. Alas, no. Not Mr Morley nor Mr Neil, either, more's the pity. No, no, it's not a pity. I'm very glad not to be deluded now. Forgive my contradictions. It's hard . . . so hard. Now, what were you asking? Ah, yes. I'm not going anywhere.

Sheila: You're not going to stay here.

Nott: I'm not going to jump in front of the London express, my dear, if that's what concerns you. I tremble now merely thinking about it.

George: Come and have a drink with us. It's more cheerful in the pub.

Nott: (*quizzically*) Duke of Wellington? The Lord Nelson?

George: Better than watching trains go by.

Nott: Oh look, the lights have changed to green. That must mean the London express is on its way. If you don't mind, I think I'll wait.

Sheila: (*to* George) Tomorrow if he's stuck he could try The Black Lion. In the Ridgeway. Though that might be full too.

(*Enter* Alf Jenkins. *He walks over the bridge from rear right towards them.*)

Nott: Black Lion? In the Ridgeway? I'll try. Thank you.

Alf: 'Ullo, 'ullo.

George: Did the committee do anything about the tickets?

Alf: Duw, the price of those tickets. To be candid, if it wasn't for the committee there'd be no loudspeakers even.

Sheila: Mr Nott, this is Alf Jenkins.

Alf: Evenin'.

Voice: (*faintly off*) Tomorrow night at Sunshine Hall. One, two, three, four, five, etc.

Nott: What's that?

Sheila: Just one of the vans advertising the Meeting.

Alf: I'm so looking forward to hearing Mr Shemtov. I've always enjoyed listening to those with the gift of the gab. I like harmonious cadence, even when it's only for vain amusement. But this is goin' to be different, mesmeric.

Nott: I don't trust any politicians.

George: This meeting tomorrow is not exactly political, it's . . . .

Alf: Goodnight, 'course it is. And there's goin' to be a big march this Easter to a place called Aldermaston. That's where they 'ave a gruesome factory for makin' H bombs. The march will have a terrific impact, almost as much as this Meeting. It'll be remembered.

George: This Meeting's nothing to do with the Bomb. The Speaker's more likely to talk about nuclear fusion than nuclear fission. How one day man will be able to harness the power of the stars.

Sheila: How do you mean, George?

George: By forcing together nuclei of hydrogen-like atoms, infinite amounts of pollution-free energy will be available.

Nott: Deuterium. Each cubic metre of sea-water contains 35 grams of deuterium.

George: What?

Nott: Supplies are limitless. The sky is limitless.

Alf: Brave New World, aye. You're a child, George, bless you.

Nott: He's right. There are supernal verities beyond narrow politics. Newton, Einstein, they sought to peer into the intimate unity of the universe. Through logic, revelation.

Alf: That's a new slogan. Through logic, revelation. I like that. Well, I better be goin'. How's your Mam, Sheila, still under the doctor?

Sheila: Just the same, Alf.

Alf: Ya. Well, 'night all. Pleased to meet you, Mr Nott.

    (*Exit* Alf *left.*)

George: Saying the Meeting's political just because he wants it to be political.

Nott: Comes a day when our critical intelligence puts such faith under a microscope and finds it counterfeit. There is nothing there but a blurred fake that once — it seems now hardly possible — prompted us to action. The sense of endeavour all in vain, argument all in vain, yes, even integrity in vain. All past display, each affirmation, now appears trivial or irrelevant — symptoms merely of our deception. Self-deception. Then looking up from the microscope we must quit the room eventually and open the front door, though we are no longer the same people who hesitate in the front porch. Now comes the challenge. We are out in the street, we must turn left or right, or cross the road. The first unfair dilemma, the first all-important decision — and we are defeated hopelessly, for we have just learnt that all directions are an illusion. We are left with a taste of nothing on the tongue and nowhere to go.

Sheila: We'd better move on, George. Are you coming to the pub with us, Mr Nott? We'll have to hurry or it'll soon be closing time.

Nott: Wait a minute. A train is coming. Would you mind very much if we waited till the train has passed?

George: It's getting late.

Nott: I don't want to inconvenience you. And you have been very kind talking to me.

George: Are you sure . . . you are Mr Nott? You're quite certain you haven't come down to address a meeting?

Sheila: George!

Nott: Just one train, please. It'll only delay you a minute.

Sheila: You don't intend jumping from that parapet?

Nott: I told you, I haven't the spunk to do that. Please stay.

(Nott *jumps on to the parapet.*)

Sheila: Come down, Mr Nott.

Nott: Look, there it is in the distance. See the lights.

George: Mr Nott, Mr Nott, do come . . .

Nott: The London Express.

George: Quick, go and get Alf.

Sheila: There isn't time. Do something George.

Nott: It's coming. It's coming.

George: Get off there. Get down you bloody fool. (*pulls at his leg*)

Nott: If only I had the courage of Mr Neil or Mr Dixon or Mr Morley.

George:(*shouting*) The train will kill you.

Nott:(*shouting*) Let go of my leg. Let go.

Sheila: Please, Mr Nott, please.

Nott: I just have to shut my eyes and fall forward.

George:(*yelling*) Come down. Come down.

(*Noise of the train becomes louder and louder and drowns the voices of* George *and* Sheila *begging Mr Nott to come down. As the train goes beneath the bridge the noise is at its greatest volume. The noise of the train gradually fades away.*)

Nott: I told you I hadn't the courage.

(*He gets down from the parapet.* George *helps him.*)

Sheila: You gave me a fright.

Nott: Mr Neil, Mr Dixon, Mr Morley — they weren't cowards. They could have done it. Not me. But Neil, Dixon and Morley didn't want to jump down. They weren't sane, you see. They didn't apprehend reality as it really is.

George: Come on, Mr Nott. I need that drink.

Nott: Thank you so much for waiting. There's so little natural courtesy about.

(*The three exit, leaving the stage empty.*)

Nott:(*off*) The Black Lion you said.

(*Lights down.*)

Scene Two

(*Scene set as in Act Two, Scene One. Time, Friday evening. On stage:* George, Sheila, Mrs Hicks, Miss Chantry, Alf Jenkins *and* Mr Nott. *Sound of distant music.*)

George: They announced the loudspeakers would come on at 6.45. I make it 6.30 now.

Sheila: No, you're fast. It's only twenty past.

Nott: I make it it five and twenty past.

Alf: That band is playing its 'eart out.

Chantry: I don't think playing military music at a time like this is appropriate. That sort of music makes me think of pools of blood and pyres of fire. I daresay I could make myself like brass bands if I tried. But I don't like trying to make myself like things.

Alf: What she want? Duke Ellington?

Chantry: (*frostily*) Why not?

Alf: Can't imagine Betty Chantry likin' jazz ha ha ha. Can't imagine . . .

Chantry: If I may say so you have very little imagination.

George: Whoops.

Chantry: You think simply because I'm a Christian in this too secular world and because I happen to be middle-aged and unmarried that Louis Armstrong and Duke Ellington and Nat King Cole and all those other brilliant black musicians are not my cup of tea. You really think I should wear sandals, don't you, never eat meat and be, I don't know, an attenuated freak.

Sheila: I'm sure Alf didn't mean anything personal, Miss Chantry.

Alf: What are you losin' your 'ead about?

Sheila: You just surprised him, that's all. You often surprise people, Miss Chantry, and that's rather wonderful.

(*Pause.*)

Chantry: I'm sorry.

Alf: Mmmm?

Chantry: I'm sorry. This is no time for bickering and smallmindedness.

Alf: I'm not bickering. I only 'ope that when those loudspeakers come on no bloody noisy train comes through. I want to hear Mr Shemtov loud and clear.

Mrs Hicks: That journalist said his name was Shapur. Whatever his real name he didn't come round, and Bill is depressed. I'm really worried. As if he's in mourning.

Sheila: He'll be O.K., Mrs Hicks.

George: At the library this morning I did a bit of research about that name, Shemtov. In the Ukraine in the early eighteenth century there was a sort of saint, a Jewish orthodox saint who was called by his disciples, listen to this, the Baal-Shem-Tov which means the Master of the Good Name. He became the founder of Hassidism. Shemtov, get it? Followers of his still exist. You must know about them, Miss Chantry? You studied comparative religion, didn't you?

Chantry: All their teaching emphasizes the importance of joy, ecstasy even. This is supposed to lead to wonder. I was taken once to one of their prayer meetings. It was in Leeds, I happened to be in Leeds a long time ago — I wasn't with Harry. It was very

53

foreign, they sang, they chanted, they jumped up and down. They closed their eyes as if hypnotised. What happened, I think, was a temporary annihilation of the self. I didn't feel anything myself. It was all rather strange. They became still, so still, yes very still indeed and then their leader held forth hinting at the profound secret of all creation.

Alf: That sounds wild.

Mrs Hicks: I think his name is Shapur not Shemtov.

Chantry: They taught that evil only exists as a lack, that it is simply God's exile. They believed nothing, nothing at all is unworthy of our love. That bit's quite Christian, isn't it? I'm reminded of a line from a poem I like: "there's nothing so small but your tenderness paints it large on a background of gold".

Sheila: Oh, that's nice.

Alf: So the original Shemtov was a religious nut?

George: He exalted music over prayer. He spoke in aphorisms and parables.

Chantry: Like our Lord.

Nott: People get things wrong all the time.

Alf: They do that. Know that story about Dr Franklin, the chap who invented the harmonica? He didn't let his wife know about the instrument till 'e got it sounding absolutely right. Then 'e played it in the bedroom at 2 o'clock in the morning. Can you imagine it? His wife asleep and Dr Franklin sitting in the dark playin' this new instrument so that she gradually wakes up and thinks, "My God, I'm hearing the music of the angels". Ha ha ha. Expect like so many women, Miss Chantry she 'ad a religious turn of mind an' so got it wrong.

Chantry: You're never very kind to women when you speak about them.

Alf: Me?

Chantry: I've noticed.

Mrs Hicks: Pity that Welsh girl you used to play tennis with emigrated to Australia. I liked her.

Alf: Yes, well now she's gone there's not a decent bit of crumpet in this town. (*pause*) Present company excepted, of course.

(Miss Chantry *looks startled.*)

George: You said just now when I told you the Master of the Good Name spoke in parables — you said, 'Like our Lord.' Like our Lord, Jesus the Anointed.

Chantry: So?

George: It's only that Baal-Shem-Tov is also supposed to have performed miracles, cured the sick by touching them. And just as Jesus saved a fallen woman, Baal Shem-Tov saved a whore. Unlike Jesus though he got married twice.

Sheila: What are you getting at, George?

George: I'm just puzzled. What we need is someone with a cosmic vision of the future not a backward prescription to dance and sing.

Alf: Who's arguing?

Nott: To know little is to know too much.

Mrs Hicks: You should have been more forward with that Welsh girl. Then she wouldn't have gone off to Australia.

Alf: Tell you the truth, Mrs Hicks, she was a bit of a tart.

(Enter Mr Jay from left on his way to the Meeting.)

Mrs Hicks: Oh, there you are, Mr Jay. I thought you said the Speaker was coming to stay with us.

Jay: So he will. The train from London came in late.

Alf: You should tell that to Bill 'icks. He's really down in the dumps.

Jay: Everything's going to be fine.

George: None of us could get any tickets.

Jay: You'll hear his speech on the tannoy. I'm not sure this is the best place, mind.

Sheila: It's packed down there.

Mrs Hicks: My husband is so disappointed, Mr Jay.

Chantry: So are we all.

Jay: Why? The Speaker'll come straight to Number 1 Shelley Street after the meeting. True, I assumed he'd come before. I didn't know the train would be so late. That's all there is to it. As for your husband's article, it'll be a beauty. The Night the Speaker Stayed at My Home. By Bill Hicks.

Mrs Hicks: I've given his room a good clean out and I've changed the curtains. If he does come, I hope it'll suit.

Nott: There's no Speaker. That's just a dream.

Chantry: What on earth are you saying?

Alf: Who are you, anyway? Hangin' around us all the time . . .

George: Leave him alone. He's not too well. *(to Jay)* Have you any spare tickets?

Jay: Just one Press ticket I'm afraid. It's a helluva thing, isn't it?

55

Look down there. All the way to the Square. All those people, some expecting a political panacea, the sick expecting new health, the poor hoping for riches.

George: Couldn't you get us in with your influence?

Chantry: Nearly thirty years I've waited.

Jay: Alas . . .

Alf: They're selling £2 tickets for thirty filthy quid . . . . Duw, what a racket. Put that in your paper.

Jay: It'll be a privilege to be inside the Hall. It's exciting. I'm excited myself. I've covered lots of highlights in my time — the Manchester United crash, the Boko Siamese twins story, you name it. I mean a moment comes, a rare precious moment in history when a door swings back wonderfully and we step out from the old into the new.

(Hum of voices and crackling from the loudspeaker.)

Chantry: Oh, I think we ought to pray.

Voice through loudspeaker: Good Evening, Good Evening, Ladies and Gentlemen, Good Evening. This is your chairman, Sir Harold Tanner. For those unfortunate enough not to be inside Sunshine Hall, your attention please. The speech from the Speaker will be relayed at seven o'clock. We expect him to arrive at any moment.

(Invisible crowd distantly sings 'Abide with Me'.)

Alf: That's better, a bit of singing.

Chantry: Isn't it thrilling, Mrs Hicks? My heart is thumping.

George: Well, this seems like it, Sheila.

Mrs Hicks: I hope Mr Jay's right and he'll come back home afterwards.

Alf: Abide with me. Very nice. Like the Cup Final.

George: Not like at Cardiff Arms Park though, eh?

Alf: Aye, that's something different. Our anthem's half a dirge and half a battle cry. Funny, when I 'ear them singing that, I can't help it, but I feel my throat tighten and tears come into my eyes. Daft, I suppose.

(From off stage now is a chorus of shouting. One man shouts, 'What do I hear?' and others respond, 'Ab. Ben. Ruach. ACadsh. Ab. Ben Ruach ACadsh.' Then the leader asks again, 'What do I hear?' and the chorus respond with the same abracadabra. They come on stage as a procession. They are going to the Meeting. They carry banners on which are written 'Welcome to the Speaker';

'Against a Dead Planet'; 'Hands off Guatemala'; and oddly 'No more Primal Darkening' and 'Not Asceticism but Joy'. At the tail end of the procession follows a spiv. The procession exits but he stays on stage.)

Offstage: What do I hear?

Off: *(with Chantry joining in)* Ab. Ben. Ruach. ACadsh. Ab Ben Ruach. ACadsh.

Spiv: Oo wants a ticket. £3 ticket dead in the centre with all the toffs. Oo's my darlin'?

George: How much?

Spiv: My very last ticket for you, my son, £80. £70, then. I'm givin' it away.

Mrs Hicks: We'll all hear from the loudspeaker.

Spiv: Speech of the century. Lissen, lissen. *(to George)* You can 'ave it for 60, okay?

George: 60?

Spiv: I'm 'ardly makin' anything on that. I 'ad to buy it so much over the odds meself. God make me blind if I'm telling you a lie.

Alf: Let's have a look at it.

Spive: It's all right, cock, it's not forged. 60 quid, 'ow's that?

Alf: I can't afford that.

Spiv: Don't waste my time. What about you, lady?

Chantry: Go away, please.

Spiv: 60 quid for the best seat in the house. You'll be sitting next to the Archbishop of Canterbury, betcher.

Chantry: You're asking a large profit on a £3 ticket. You ought to be reported.

(Enter man right.)

Spiv: All right — since it's getting so near 7 o'clock you can 'ave it for 55. A give away.

Man: 50. I'll give you 50.

Spiv: You must be joking. This is Row D. Dead centre.

Man: Take it or leave it.

Spiv: All right, all right. I'm cripplin' meself. Never mind. Be good to other people, that's what I allers say. Please the punters, that's my motto.

Man: Seven, eight, nine, ten.

Spiv: Fivers, right. There you are. Enjoy yourself.

(Exit man.)

Nott: Some people are so stupid.

57

Mrs Hicks: It's time the loudspeakers came on.

George: I hope there's no hitch.

Alf: I know people who've paid a fortune for a ticket at Twickenham but this is ridiculous. There was a chap, Davies-Each Way we called him who paid . . .

Spiv: (*pulling out ticket from pocket*) Last ticket. Very last ticket.

George: You said the other one was your last.

Spiv: This is my own ticket. Oo you tryin' to catch? Swear to you it's my last one. God blind me if it's not my last one.

Chantry: You shouldn't tempt fate like that.

Spiv: I've sixty-sixty vision still, 'aven't I? Listen, 40 for my last ticket. Rock bottom that is.

George: I'll give you 40 for two tickets.

Sheila: No, George, no.

Spiv: That's a laugh. Anyway I ain't got two tickets. 40 for one ticket, take it or leave it . . . (*pause*)

> (*Begins to exit.*)

Chantry: Good riddance to bad . . .

George: (*calling*) 30 pounds.

Sheila: For heaven's sake, no. (*angry and loud*) For Chrissake, George.

Spiv: All right, I'm robbin' myself, but all right. You're Scrooge, you are.

Sheila: You can't, George. You promised me. He promised me, Mrs Hicks.

George: I want to go. I've got to go. I want so much to be there.

Mrs Hicks: Don't be silly, George.

Sheila: Last night you said, like snow, you said before . . . .

Mrs Hicks: You hear me? You're not to do it. Where did you get that money from?

Spiv: Lady, please, lady. Yes or no, yes or no?

Alf: You'll hear it from the tannoy, mun.

Spiv: I'll give you three before I double my price. One two, ah ta.

Nott: It's sad, so very sad, to see what people will do just to hear the howl of a shaman, the mutterings of some deluded charismatic.

Sheila: (*sad*) You're impossible, George Hicks, you're too much trouble. Once yes, twice yes, but this.

George: Look. You can have the ticket. If you want. You go, yes you go.

Sheila: Yes, I'll go.

(*Exit* Sheila *swiftly.*)

George: (*calling*) Sheila. Sheila.

Mrs Hicks: Go after her, son.

Spiv: Nah then. Oo wants balloons? (*takes them out of pocket*) Red white and blue balloons. Half a dollar each. Guaranteed not to bust.

(*Shrugs his shoulders and then exits.*)

Spiv: (*off*) Greet the Speaker with patriotic balloons.

Alf: Well, er, you'll 'ave to be sharp if you're going. It's nearly seven. Mind you, if you feel you should go after Sheila I understand.

Mrs Hicks: He should, he certainly should.

Alf: Shame to waste the ticket though. I mean if you're not using it, George, I'll . . . er . . .

Chantry: You'll be in Row D. You'll be that close to him.

Nott: You might be able to resell that ticket. Down there I expect there are other mugs.

George: I did offer it to her, mother. Damn it all. It's once in a lifetime.

(*Exit* George.)

Nott: Damn fool.

Mrs Hicks: He's a good boy really. I know my son through and through. Who's not a little selfish? He's young, impetuous . . . . Maybe he'll bring the Speaker back home with him.

Alf: With money you can buy everything. People with money, most of them, they disgust me.

Chantry: Never mind, we'll all hear him here. That's all that counts. To hear his voice that should be enough for any of us. You don't have to see him. You don't even have to see a photograph of him — any more than you do all the people in the bible.

Alf: It's all wrong, you know. People making profit on things like that.

Mrs Hicks: It's time. It's seven o'clock.

Chantry: And there's the loudspeakers coming on.

Alf: This is it. Think of it. They'll be reading about this Meeting all over the world.

Voice Over Loudspeaker: Citizens!

Alf: This is it.

59

Voice Over Loudspeaker: I'm afraid we must apologise, citizens.

Chantry: What's wrong?

Voice Over Loudspeaker: Ladies and Gentlemen, I regret to inform you the Speaker has not arrived.

Alf: Hear that?

Voice Over Loudspeaker: Meantime I've asked one of the organisers to say a few words.

Chantry: Not arrived?

Mrs Hicks: There must be some mistake.

Voice Over Loudspeaker: Here he is. Could we have your applause please?

    (*Silence.*)

A round of applause please?

Alf: They're stunned in the Hall.

Mrs Hicks: They're not even booing.

Second Voice Over Loudspeaker: Ladies and Gentlemen, One two three four five six seven.

Mass Voices Over Loudspeaker: Boo! Get off! Boo! Boo! Out out out!

Alf: Now they're booing all right.

First Voice Over Loudspeaker: Please Citizens, Please. Silence please.

Mass Voices: Out Out Out Out!

Second Voice Over Loudspeaker: And one two three four five six seven.

Mrs Hicks: What's he saying?

Second Voice Over Loudspeaker: And seven six five four three two one.

Mass Voices: Boo! Boo Boo Boo etc.

Alf: They're not saying anything. The Speaker has not arrived.

Second Voice: And one two three.

    (*Loudspeaker crackles and the voices abruptly end. Silence.*)

Nott: It's broken down, the loudspeaker system has failed.

Chantry: Or someone in the Hall sabotaged it. We're going to miss the Speaker.

Alf: He hasn't turned up.

Mrs Hicks: Listen, the band has started to play again.

    (*There is a faint distant sound of military music.*)

Nott: He's not going to turn up. He'll never turn up.

Mrs Hicks: I want to go home. I don't want to stay here any more.

Alf: He's got to turn up.

Chantry: Just late, that's all.

Mrs Hicks: Come home with me, Miss Chantry.

Chantry: Never, never.

Alf: (*to* Nott) But it's impossible, the advertisements, the announcements.

Nott: Once I too felt I was pursued by demons and longed for a new Messiah.

Alf: What?

> (*Enter* George.)

Mrs Hicks: George?

Alf: You're back quick.

George: Thirty quid down the drain. The ticket was a fraud.

Nott: So was the Speaker a fraud.

Alf: I've had enough of you, mate. Get out of it.

Nott: I'm telling you the truth.

Chantry: He blasphemes. Hit him, Alf, hit him, hit him hard.

> (Alf *moves forward threateningly*.)

Nott: (*screams rapidly*) One two three four five six seven one two three four five . . . .

George: (*shouts*) Don't hurt him.

Mrs Hicks: No, don't hurt him.

Alf: 'E's asked for it.

Nott: One two three four five . . . .

Chantry: Shut up, shut up.

Nott: Six seven one two three four . . . .

> (Alf *slaps him across the face*.)

Nott: five six seven ha ha ha ha ha.

> (Nott *is suddenly quiet*. Miss Chantry *takes out a handkerchief and blows her nose*.)

Mrs Hicks: There, there, dear.

Chantry: If only Harry were here.

George: Sheila . . . Sheila didn't come back?

Nott: Dreams. Bloody, gaudy dreams. Don't you think that I want to believe that there's a Speaker too? And you (*to* George) you're not in love with that girl, Sheila.

George: What do you mean?

Nott: You merely want to escape from the greyness of all this.

Like the others. There are many ways to leave. I took another door even less satisfactory. But if your heart had been genuinely touched, you would yearn for nothing, having all. There is no one so courageous as one who loves.

Alf: I wouldn't stand for that sort of talk, boy.

Nott: (*bullying*) And you, too.

Alf: Me?

Nott: And you (*points to* Mrs Hicks) and you (*points to* Miss Chantry) all of you — have no courage. No more than I have, or had. If you had, then everything would be so good — well, at least, better. You wouldn't have to search for any public orthodoxy, or build a cocoon of dreams, or any false structure to feel safe in, to lie in — there'd be just the green, cruel, ordinary world that indisputably is, and you'd praise that difficult simplicity.

Alf: No.

Nott: It's as if you say "no" out of habit.

Alf: I'm goin'. I'm not listening to 'im.

(Some of the crowd come on to the bridge from the direction of Sunshine Hall muttering ad lib, e.g. "they made a proper Charlie out of us", "A real frost", "Bloody fraud", etc.)

Mrs Hicks: Are you coming, George?

(Alf *begins to exit.*)

Nott: You all wanted to hear the Speaker, didn't you?

Alf: He's a nut.

Chantry: I don't want to listen to that man any more.

(The crowd on the bridge have begun to listen with interest to the proceedings.)

Nott: Come back. I'll tell you what the Speaker would have said. Come back and listen.

Alf: (*turning back*) 'Ere boys, 'ere's a bloke what says he knows.

George: Leave him alone. Leave him be.

Crowd: Ya Ya.

Nott: He'd say it's time we stopped deluding ourselves. It's time to accept.

Alf:(*mockingly*) Hear, HEAR.

Nott: (*becoming more and more fantastic and rhetorical as his speech continues*) To accept even our own terror of ignorance, this here and now, this time, this earth, this most strange of meeting places.

Alf and Several: Hear HEAR. Hear HEAR.

(*The crowd, interested, come closer to him to listen.* Nott *continues his soapbox speech with his back to the audience. The faces and gestures of the crowd become more and more menacing as* Nott *carries on with his oratory.*)

Nott: We don't want any hysterical formulae for the future. We don't want 'was' or 'will be'. We want 'is'.

Alf and All The Crowd: Hear HEAR hear HEAR hear HEAR.

Nott: (*very phoney and theatrical*) I don't want to listen to another time's sad messages of 'Love', 'Obey', 'War', 'Peace', 'Vote'.

Alf and All The Crowd: HEAR hear. HEAR hear. HEAR hear. HEAR hear.

Nott:(*even more wildly*) No more tell me of the rose's waste. I see our eyes move into a different love. I see our heart forget the Night's infirmary.

Alf and Crowd: (their rhythmical 'Hear hears' now gradually begin to imitate the sound made by a train*) Hear-hear, Hear-hear, Hear-hear, Hear-hear.*

Nott: (*raving*) What value is the grave bedecked with flowers?

Crowd: (*during his speech*) Hear-hear, Hear-hear, Hear-hear, Hear-hear.

Nott: (*making himself heard above the din*) Don't you know the Speaker is the future? When we're perfect he'll be here. Here!

Crowd: Hear-hear, hear-hear, hear-hear, hear-hear.

Nott: (*his voice almost drowned by the menacing chant*) Don't you know . . .

Crowd: Hear-hear, hear-hear, hear-hear, hear-hear, hear-hear, hear-hear.

Nott: Listen to me. Listen to . . .

Crowd: Hear hear, hear-hear, hear-hear, hear-hear, hear-hear, hear-hear, hear-hear, hear-hear, hear-hear. etc.

(Nott *puts his hands over his ears, terrified as the chant of train-like'hear-hears' continues. Superimposed now on the 'hear-hears' is the actual sound of a train coming towards the bridge. With the engine's whistle this rises to a crescendo.* Nott *falls down and all is silent.*)

Nott: (*quietly*) Don't you know that the Speaker is the future?

(*All on stage, feeling perhaps they've gone too far in baiting* Nott, *exit quickly. Only* George *remains. He helps* Nott *to his feet.*)

Nott: When we're all perfect, he will have arrived.

(*Lights down.*)

ACT THREE

(Scene as in Act One. Time, later Friday evening. On stage, Mr
Hicks, George, Alf Jenkins *and* Miss Chantry. Hicks *and* George
are playing a game of chess.)

Hicks: *(turning to* Alf) If that journalist comes here again I'll do
him.

Alf: Quite right.

Hicks: Promising all manner of things. They'd murder their own
mothers for the sake of half a column.

George: Come on, Dad, your move. You always go off on a
tangent when you're losing.

Alf: I just fail to understand why the Speaker didn't come.

Chantry: It was a mistake, that's all. We just have to wait, keep
faith. Perhaps it was our faith that was being tested? Like Job in
the bible.

Alf: She's got 'er sermon face on again.

Hicks: What did you hope for anyway? I had a damn good reason
for wanting the Speaker to turn up, none of this airy-fairy stuff.

Chantry: I hoped for the dissipation of doubt. I hoped for
evidence of my faith, I longed for a revelation that would refresh
us all. How arrogant of me. It was my pride that was speaking.

Alf: Honestly, Miss Chantry. I have to tell you you're getting
worse. You can hardly open your mouth these days without
sounding like a religious broadcast.

Chantry: You don't have to be so rude.

Alf: You're more screwy than that feller on the bridge.

George: Easy Alf.

Chantry: I don't need your protection, George.

Alf: That bloke on the bridge made me tampin' mad. Where did
he go to anyway?

George: He has a friend in the town. Went looking for him. He
wasn't so crazy. I wish to hell I'd listened to him and stayed with
Sheila instead of chasing moonbeams.

Hicks: There!

George: You can't castle, Dad. My bishop's covering that square.

Hicks: Oh.

Alf: Somebody must know the way out. The Speaker would have told us.

Chantry: He would have done.

Alf: For me and millions of others whose work it is to put something by 'ere, fold something by there, minute in, minute out, only to have the monotony relieved by kicking a lever down once every quarter of an hour. I ask you — is such repetitive labour fit for the dignity of human beings with brains and hearts and souls?

Chantry: It's better than being unemployed.

Alf: Is it?

Hicks: Auto-mation, auto-mation, that's what they need.

George: Are you playing or not?

Alf: Not even socialism is the answer. We're ruddy robots, that's what we are. Where's the satisfaction in working, looking at the telly, sleeping, doing boring work again an' 'aving a week or two's holiday in Blackpool or Bridlington or Margate in the rain and then going back to work again?

Chantry: A job you enjoy is important. I can't say I enjoy working in a chartered surveyor's office.

Alf: Where's the spiritual joy? Where's the system that do give an answer? What political party talks about the needs of a man's mind as well as his belly? Where's the flowerin' and the dancin' and the stamping energy of joy? Where's the imaginative delight?

Chantry: Yes.

Alf: Aye, we need the Speaker.

Chantry: Yes, you're right.

Alf: We need a new political prophet. We need a new political philosophy. There was Karl Marx in the nineteenth century but now it's the mid-twentieth century and where's the answer?

Chantry: Religion is the answer and the way.

Alf: Oh Gawd.

George: If it's someone like Hitler you're talking about, some demagogue like that, then you're up the pole.

Hicks: There, mind your queen.

Alf: I didn't mean anyone like that. Course not. Not somebody tawdry and pathological like that. But it's a vision of a just society we need beyond the small triumphs of intermittent occasions. Our so-called statesmen could destroy the world, make a radioactive cemetery out of this planet.

George: Check.

Alf: 'itler, my God. As if I was thinkin' of someone like 'itler.

Chantry: You don't really believe the Son of God walked on this earth two thousand years ago, do you, Mr Jenkins? If you did, you'd accept there could be a Second Coming — one accepted by Christians as Christ, by Jews as the Messiah, by Moslems as the Imam Mahdi and by Buddhists as the fifth Buddha.

Alf: Struth.

George: It's check.

Hicks: I know it's check. Where's your mother? My chest feels very tight tonight.

Chantry: She's having a little lie down.

Hicks: I could do with a hot drink. It would help. Hear me wheeze?

George: I said check.

Hicks: Check check check, I know. I can see the board. My chest is bad but my eyes are all right.

(*There is a ring at the front doorbell.* George *rising knocks over the board.*)

George: That's Sheila.

Hicks: Look what you've done. You deliberately knocked the board over.

(George *exits hurriedly through door left.*)

(*to* Alf *and* Miss Chantry) I was murderin' him and he knocks the board over, Christ! Give me a cigarette, Alf.

Chantry: You've given it up.

Hicks: It'll clear me chest. A fag'll clear it.

Alf: I don't think I should.

Hicks: I'll just take three puffs, honest. Just to clear the tubes. Aw, come on, Alf.

Chantry: You swore you wouldn't ever smoke again. That was your New Year's resolution.

Hicks: What you want, Alf? Me to go on my knees?

Alf: Don't tell the missus I gave it to you.

Hicks: Ta.

(Hicks *lights up.*)

Chantry: My New Year's resolution was not to talk about religion so much. I've not done very well either.

Alf: There's nothing wrong in talkin' about what interests you. Bill talks about himself all the time, see. Ha ha.

Hicks: Immediately after the war in Germany, in 1945, you could get yourself a woman, so they say, wiv one of these.

(*Enter* George *with* Mr Jay.)

Jay: Hello! What a fiasco! A sensation, the Speaker mistaking the date like that.

Chantry: Mistake?

Alf: What happened? Tell us what happened.

Jay: He didn't turn up.

Hicks: I'll say he didn't turn up. You've got some explaining to do. My wife spent hours . . . .

George: (*near door left*) I'm going to look for Sheila.

Jay: You're not going to wait for the Speaker? Didn't you know? When the tannoy system broke down, they announced in the Hall that the Speaker had been detained.

(*Enter* Mrs Hicks. Bill Hicks *immediately puts out his cigarette.*)

But he would come tomorrow.

Mrs. Hicks: Tomorrow?

Jay: Probably he'll turn up tonight. He might already be here, in the town.

Alf: Unavoidably detained! Doesn't sound as if 'e 'ad much consideration for people.

Chantry: Look at them! Look at the circus they tried to make of it. The black market in tickets. The spivvery and rowdyism. We weren't pure enough for him today. I understand. I understand very well. Let's hope we won't all be so foolish tomorrow.

Hicks: You don't really think he's going to come tomorrow.

Jay: Of course. Why do you think I'm here?

George: Go on. Tell them all there's no Speaker. No Mr Shemtov. No Mr Shapur, or whatever his name is will be coming here. Why lie? Why keep up the pretence?

Mrs Hicks: Don't be so rude to our guest, George.

George: You know, Dad. You were sceptical from the beginning. Tell them once and for all — tell him to get out and stop tormenting us with phoney promises.

Hicks: Now, now, not so hasty, lad. Maybe there's something in it. Mr Jay here's from London. He's come all this way — not for nothing, surely?

George: If Sheila comes, Mum, tell her I've gone to look for her. I won't be long.

Jay: Young generation walks out as Speaker is due.

George: Stop talking in bloody silly headlines.

(*Exit* George.)

Mrs Hicks: I'm sorry, Mr Jay.

Jay: Oh, that's all right. He's young, he's earnest. A nice boy like that, I like him.

(*Sound of* George *forcibly banging door offstage.*)

Hicks: The putty'll come off that door. We've got coloured glass in that front door. Won't be easy to replace. You speak to 'im about slamming doors, Doris.

Chantry: We should be happy. Mr Jay has brought good news.

Jay: Mr Hicks. I'll make a prophecy. I don't say it lightly, mind you. I'm weighing my words carefully. He won't come here tomorrow.

Chantry: Oh.

Hicks: You're dead right for a change.

Jay: He'll come here tonight. As I said, he's probably in the town already. That's why I'm here now because I bet he'll be in this house tonight. Scores of important people came off the last London train including your CND lot — Fenner Brockway, Canon Collins, Michael Foot, Frank Cousins.

Alf: Are you trying to tell us . . . ?

Chantry: Faith, Mr Jenkins.

Jay: I'd better start getting notes for your article, Mr Hicks.

Hicks: I have a bad chest. At night, when I wake up ready to pee I can hardly catch my breath and I get frightened.

Jay: Yes, yes. I'll get that in.

Hicks: I'm not tellin' you my medical 'istory for any bloody article. I'm trying to say you shouldn't mislead an ailing man like me.

Jay: I must know more about the boarders in this house. Do you mind me asking you where you were born?

Alf: Mind your own bloody business.

Chantry: Mr Jenkins was born in South Wales. Very crude.

Alf: I was born in Porthcawl in 1917. In the nude, if you must know.

Mrs Hicks: Tell him about yourself, Alf. What's it matter anyway?

Alf: Aw, it's all silly, Mrs Hicks.

Jay: What did your father do, Mr Jenkins?

Alf: Dad? He was killed November 1918. Last bullet fired almost. Aye, the dammed idiot gettin' mixed up in that Imperialist war. Mam 'ad a sweet shop in Porthcawl. When I was a nipper I wasn't short of bullseyes, acid drops, mintoes, oh no I wasn't.

Jay: Porthcawl. The seaside resort?

Alf: Windy place. Sand dunes. Esplanade. There's a legend, you know, about a lost soul wandering the dunes near Porthcawl uttering terrible wailing cries. It used to frighten the 'ell out of me that story when I was a kid.

Jay: That's very . . . er . . . interesting.

Alf: Mam 'ad a cancer of the larynx when I was eleven an' I became an errand boy.

Hicks: Didn't know that, Alf.

Alf: Oh aye. I liked cycling, see. They let me ride a bike being an errand boy.

Chantry: I expect you whistled all the time.

Alf: Not like you. Do you know her party piece? She whistles and juggles three lemons at the same time. She did it for us last Christmas. Right, Mrs Hicks?

Chantry: My father taught me how to juggle when I was so high. Last Christmas I drank too much.

Alf: I had an uncle in Treorchy. He got me a job there, in a bicycle shop. It was an 'appy time that. 'Elping to sell Rudges and Raleighs, Royal Enfields, Humbers and Hudsons. Then there was the old B.S.A and the Sunbeams and Hercules.

Chantry: I had a Raleigh.

Alf: I was just a boy, you know. Then bang came the depression and the Prince of Wales came down and says, "Something must be done." People couldn't afford bikes then. Eighteen years old and unemployed so I came north but didn't 'ave the fare to go all the way so stopped off by here. Saturday it was an' I saw an ad for factory workers. Been 'ere ever since. I was a conchie during the war. Aye, I said no to that.

Jay: Didn't you get married?

Alf: I said No to that too. I'm too fly for that, boy. I never got trapped.

Jay: No story to touch the heart perhaps?

Alf: Sob story? She's got one. Ask her about Harry Wallace.

Jay: Nothing else you want to tell me?

Alf: (*smiling*) When I was a kid at school you know, I used to sing with all the others. "Let the prayer re-echo, God Bless the Prince of Wales." I thought they were saying, for years, "Prairie echo" an' I was wonderin' where the 'ell were the prairies in Wales, ha ha.

Hicks: Ah. Ha ha ha. Prairie echo. That's a good one.

Jay: Who's Harry Wallace?

Alf: Harry Wallace an' 'er were goin' to get married.

Mrs Hicks: Oh no, leave it.

Chantry: I should like to tell him about Harry and myself, Mrs Hicks. Why shouldn't I?

Jay: Please. Sit down. Tell me.

Hicks: We all know it off by heart. Christ.

Chantry: It was a long time ago. There was family opposition. I was only nineteen and my father thought he knew better. So we eloped, hoping of course my father would relent. We were very happy until Harry died in a fire, three months later.

Jay: A fire?

Chantry: We were in the street, walking arm in arm. We turned a corner and there above a shop was a window with a woman and a child shouting for help. The whole building was raging with straw-coloured flames. On the pavement below, a group of people had gathered, but didn't do anything and at that time the firemen hadn't arrived.

Mrs Hicks: Don't upset yourself again, Miss Chantry. Every time you tell it you get so upset.

Chantry: (*as if in a trance*) My Harry went into that Nebuchadnezzar's furnace. He went in like Shadrach, Meshach and Abed-nego. But no angel interceded. My darling ran back into the street ripping his clothes off. He wasn't a man any more. He was a human torch. I could smell his burning skin, the odour of charred meat. "Harry," I shouted, "Harry, Harry." Nobody did anything. "Help my Harry," I screamed, but nobody could do anything. I saw his eyes staring into my eyes. I'll never forget his eyes, never. The imploring, hopeless gaze.

Mrs Hicks: It's time, love, you put it out of your mind.

71

Chantry: (*suddenly screams*) Harry, Harry. For pity's sake. Don't leave me, Harry.

Alf: There, there, Betty.

Chantry: (*sobbing*) Oh, Harry, Harry. I love you so.

Mrs Hicks: Now Miss Chantry.

Chantry: I was only nineteen, Mrs Hicks. Was it fair?

Alf: (*suddenly to* Jay) You said the Speaker was going to arrive. If he don't you'll copit from us, I promise.

Mrs Hicks: Alf, what are you saying?

Hicks: It's half past nine. It's getting late for a lodger to come.

Jay: Don't worry, don't worry.

Mrs Hicks: All right, Miss Chantry?

Chantry: Thank you. I'm sorry.

Alf: You know. I once saw a girl getting on a bus. She was so beautiful. No lipstick, no make-up, no nothing, mun. She had a face like an angel. Big eyes, so sad and clear. I got on that bus though I wasn't going anywhere. I just wanted to look at her longer. I never spoke to her or anything and when she got off I just went on to the terminus, then walked home.

Jay: What about you, Mrs Hicks? Were you born here?

Mrs Hicks: Oh yes. I've lived here all my life.

Jay: And? Go on.

Mrs Hicks: Father was a schoolteacher, you know, but he went deaf. He couldn't work because of it. Like my poor husband. Mother had to help out.

Hicks: I'm not deaf, it's my chest.

Mrs Hicks: I worked as a secretary for Patterson and Son. Their offices are still near Sunshine Hall. I should have learnt languages.

Hicks: I know what's coming. Go on. Go on, tell all the world about Simon Mitchell.

Mrs Hicks: I was a pretty girl you know, and Simon Mitchell did have a crush on me.

Hicks: That was 'undreds of years ago.

Mrs Hicks: You be quiet. Surely you're not jealous now?

Hicks: Jealous? He was the lucky one.

Mrs Hicks: Simon went.

Hicks: To Italy.

Mrs Hicks: To Milan.

Hicks: (*mimicking his wife's voice*) She could have got a job in Milan. (*own voice*) Don't be so stupid in front of everybody.

Mrs Hicks: I didn't learn Italian. I stayed behind. I wasn't a very practical person.

Hicks: Don't make such a fool of yourself in front of this . . . stranger.

Mrs Hicks: Yes, I was a silly girl. I dreamed of being a famous actress like Kay Francis or Myrna Loy or Norma Shearer or Loretta Young.

Jay: You went on the stage, Mrs Hicks?

Mrs Hicks: Oh dear, no. I got as far as the local drama group, that's all. That's where I met my husband — at one of their dances. I thought he looked like a mixture of William Powell, Melvyn Douglas and Ronald Colman.

(Jay *looks at* Hicks *astonished.*)

He didn't really, it was just that he wore a moustache in those days.

Hicks: And I thought that she looked like Doris Karloff.

Chantry: It takes me right back, you talking about Raleighs and Rudges and Sunbeams, Mr Jenkins.

Alf: Good bikes. Very good bikes, all of them.

Chantry: It makes me think of a tune. I don't know why. Harry had a record. On one side was 'I've got my Captain working for me now' and on the other, 'You'd be surprised.'

Hicks: (*sings*) Da da di da da da da, dadadi da da da da, you'd be surprised.

Mrs Hicks: I remember that. (*sings*) Di di dida da da da, you'd be surprised.

Hicks: (*sings*) I'm not much of a look-er, I'm not much of a lover, but when you get me in the dark, la la la de de de deda, you'd be surprised. (*slaps his wife's bottom playfully*).

Chantry: You've got the words all wrong.

(Chantry, Hicks *and* Mrs Hicks *all sing together. Ring on the front doorbell. They stop singing and wait, not speaking for a moment, as if they just imagined that the bell had rung. Hicks stands up, looks towards the door then sits down again silently.*)

Mrs Hicks: I'll make some tea. Shall I make some tea?

Jay: The bell rang.

Alf: I'd like to go back to Porthcawl one day. See the lighthouse again and the little harbour.

Jay: I heard the bell go. It's probably the Speaker.

Alf: That was no bell.

(*Bell rings again.*)

Jay: Shall I open the door?

Chantry: (*shrill*) Who touched me?

Mrs Hicks: What?

Chantry: (*protesting*) Somebody touched me.

Mrs Hicks: Bill?

Hicks: She was nowhere near me. She was nowhere near anybody.

(Jay *moves towards door left.*)

Hicks: (*shouting*) You stay where you are, Mr Jay.

Jay: It's the Speaker. At the door.

Alf: No.

Hicks: Can't be.

Chantry: Peace be to this house.

Mrs Hicks: I'll answer it, Bill.

Hicks: Yes, whatever you say.

(*Exit* Mrs Hicks *through door left.*)

Chantry: I've a headache. Whenever my mother had a headache she used to put eau-de-cologne on her forehead. (*pause*) Did not Luke teach us, 'Nothing is impossible'?

Jay: I told you he'd come, Mr Hicks. *The Daily Star* promised and there you are.

Chantry: (*mumbles*) The latchet of whose shoes I am not worthy to unloose.

Jay: I confess I was doubtful myself. I was just keeping up your spirits but the *Star* must have found out his address and really sent that telegram.

Hicks: It may only be Sheila.

Alf: Or George coming back. He said he'd only be a few minutes.

Hicks: No, George has got a key.

Chantry: Zacharias was struck dumb for doubting his vision.

(*Enter* Mrs Hicks.)

Mrs Hicks: Come in, please.

(*Enter* Mr Nott.)

Mrs Hicks: He's looking for Mr Mason.

Jay: (*triumphantly*) There, didn't I tell you? (*shaken*) Good Lord.

Nott: Mrs Hicks tells me he died, I didn't know.

Hicks: Yes, yes. Sudden. Poor Mason.

Nott: I see we've all met before. (*to* Hicks) Except you, sir. I er . . . didn't realise you were so near the station or I would have come earlier.

Hicks: It's a corner house. This place. No 1 Shelley Street.

Nott: Mmm. I like corner houses, they're so light.

Jay: I told you.

Alf: But he's the barmy one, Bill.

Nott: Poor Mr Mason. I can hardly believe it.

Jay: I hope you have no objection to the Press? I er . . . I'm on the *Star*.

Hicks: Mason's dead all right. This is the right house.

Alf: He's an imposter.

Nott: I beg your pardon?

Alf: What's your name?

Nott: Oh . . . Nott.

Alf: Are you sure?

Nott: I sometimes used to call myself by other names.

Jay: Oh, we understand, don't we, Mr Hicks? You have several names. One must keep incognito.

Nott: How understanding of you . . . all. When we were on the bridge I feared you didn't like me.

Chantry: You are the Speaker. All the time you lingered on the bridge while they waited for you to speak in Sunshine Hall.

Nott: I don't follow you.

Alf: Are you the Speaker or no?

Nott: The Speaker? Me?

Hicks: Of course he is. Jay said he'd come and here he is. Because of Mr Mason he said and it's true.

Nott: (*rising*) No, no, there's some mistake.

Chantry: You saw that people weren't ready for you. You smelt the smell of corruption and kept your silence. I understand.

Mrs Hicks: And on the bridge you slapped his face.

Alf: He said there was no use waiting for the Speaker on the bridge.

Nott: I must go.

Hicks: Naturally. He should know if he were going to speak or not.

Jay: I must get my photographer.

Nott: Please, please everybody.

> (*Enter* George.)

Alf: Fancy it was you all the time.

Hicks: That contract, Mr Jay. My God, I'll be able to work again.

Mrs Hicks: We were all afraid but seeing you we're not afraid any more.

Nott: I must leave. I really must leave. I must find myself an hotel.

George: What's going on here?

Nott: They think I'm the Speaker.

George: The Speaker? (George *begins to laugh*) What a joke . . . the Speaker. Not Shemtov, not Shapur, but Nott, ha ha ha.

Chantry: What are you laughing at?

Alf: What's so funny?

Mrs Hicks: George!

Hicks: (*shouts*) Stop laughing!

George: Laughing? Look!

Alf: What is it?

George:(*opens his right hand*) The engagement ring, that's all. It's all off. Me and Sheila are through.

Nott: You shouldn't have bought that ticket. I'm sorry. Well . . . goodbye.

Jay: Goodbye?

Nott: Mr Mason's dead. There's no point in staying here.

Jay: No point? Everybody's waiting for you. Not just here, but out there. Everybody.

George: He's not the Speaker, you damn fool. He's just a man called Nott.

Nott: That's right. That's what I was trying to say.

George: Tell them about yourself.

Nott: Mr Mason and I. We met on holiday once. We struck up a friendship. He told me if I ever was in this town I should call on him. I apologise.

Hicks: Apologise?

Chantry: You're the Speaker.

Nott: I can identify myself. Let me see. (*pulls out papers from inside pocket*) Here's my driving licence. You see my name? Nott. And here's a letter addressed to me. (*gives it to* Jay) It's from the Superintendent of a hospital. I was very ill. I am still a little ill, if you really want to know. They said I must take it easy for a while. I'm only convalescing.

Jay: (*reading letter*) "Dear Mr Nott, You certainly have made splendid progress and it was kind of you to write to us. Certainly, come back and chat with us any time you feel you want to. Remember, life is beautiful. All you need is courage. With very good wishes, Yours faithfully."

Alf: I said he was barmy.

Jay: It's signed R.S. Braybrook, MD, DPM. A psychiatrist!

Chantry: You're the Speaker. He's lying. Can't you see?

Nott: I'm not.

Chantry: I know you're the Speaker.

Nott: You're deluded.

George: You've made a mistake, that's all, Miss Chantry.

Chantry: (*almost hysterical*) Say you're the Speaker. Tell them the truth. We've waited so long. Admit it, admit it.

Nott: Please control yourself.

Chantry: You cruel bastard. (*goes to attack him, both arms akimbo ready to strike*)

Nott: This woman. Keep her away from me.

Chantry: You have the power and the glory. But you took Harry away from me.

(Miss Chantry *attacks* Nott. George *and* Alf *intervene and hold her back.*)

(*weeping*) Let me get at him. The pig. The absolute, merciless swine.

Nott: You should face up to the truth.

George: You'd better go.

Nott: I'm very sorry about this. Yes, so sorry. Where did you say the hotel, the Black Lion was, The Ridgeway, did you say?

(*Exit* Nott *through door left.*)

Chantry: (*screams*) Don't let him leave. Please. Please come back, come back.

Alf: Easy there, sweetheart, easy.

George: We all made an error, that's all, Miss Chantry. All of us.

Hicks: (*to Jay*) Now what have you got to say?

Chantry: (*sobs*) Face up to the truth. (*covers her face with her hands*)

Jay: It seems I was wrong. But here's ten pounds, Mr Hicks, from the *Star*. You'll read about this . . . .

Hicks: (*taking ten pounds*) Get out.

Chantry: Face up to the truth? I can face up to the truth.

Mrs Hicks: Of course you can, dear. Everything's going to be all right. Go upstairs and have a lie-down.

Chantry: I'll tell you the truth. Harry Wallace . . . .

Mrs Hicks: Not now, Miss Chantry. Later.

Chantry: There was family opposition.

Mrs Hicks: I know, I know. They were very wrong. Very wrong of them.

Chantry: No, they were right.

Alf: Right?

Chantry: You see, my father knew something I didn't. He knew that Harry was a married man and had three children.

Alf: You never told us that.

Chantry: Harry never told me that. My father told me the facts. Harry's left hand was under my head and his right hand embraced me but he didn't tell me he was married. I left home and never saw him again.

Mrs Hicks: What about the fire?

Chantry: There was no fire. I wished there had been a fire. He cheated me. He cooed like in the Song of Solomon — "Stay me with flagons, comfort me with apples for I am sick with love." He lied. When he dies I hope the flames of hell burn him up. May they scorch his flesh. May he remain in perpetual torment as I have been all these years.

(*Exit through door rear right. There is a long pause.*)

Jay: What's that noise? Outside?

Alf: I didn't hear anything.

George: Just a dog howling in the night.

Mrs Hicks: Poor Miss Chantry.

Alf: Well. All the time she 'ad me fooled 'bout that fire. Women, you can't trust them.

Hicks: Ah, you've no call to throw stones.

Alf: What do you mean? What you drivin' at?

Hicks: We all know women aren't up your street.

Alf: What are you talkin' about? I get lonely sometimes. Yes, I admit that. I do get very lonely.

Mrs Hicks: There, there Bill.

Hicks: It's all very well to say "there, there" but do you realise what we've lost?

Jay: I don't know what to say.

Alf: (*to* Jay) 'alf the time 'e talks bloody rubbish.

Mrs Hicks: (*to* Hicks) What's it matter anyway?

Hicks: Matter? My taxi's gone, that's all. A chance to earn a dignified living.

Mrs Hicks: Even if you got the car you wouldn't have used it for a taxi. You would have sat right in that chair and George would have driven the car around.

Hicks: What are you saying? You're stupid. My chest would've allowed me to do that.

Mrs Hicks: You know the doctor told you it's mainly nerves, umpteen times. So what's the point of making a big song and dance about that car?

Alf: That's very interestin'. Ho ho.

Hicks: That doctor's just a quack. You know that. You know how sometimes I can hardly breathe. Nerves, rubbish. It's you who's got a nerve fabricating stories like that. Don't listen to 'er, Alf. Isn't my chest bad, son?

(*Coughs and gasps.*)

George: You know mother's right. Let's face up to the truth, all of us.

Hicks: You're an idiot too. No wonder Sheila threw 'im over.

George: That last job you had, when you ripped off the cash Sir Harold Tanner gave you for tyres.

Hicks: That was a misunderstanding.

Mrs Hicks: Leave him alone, George, what's the use?

George: Why should we leave him alone? Sheila and I would be married by now instead of in this mess. You take in lodgers and I have to give you money instead of being able to save enough to put down on a house. Life could be beautiful, that doctor said in the letter.

Hicks: I did my best.

George: When you worked for that car hire firm before the job with Sir Harold . . . .

Hicks: I have nothing to be ashamed of there. It was the boss's son. It would have been all right if it hadn't been . . . .

George: And before that? At the cinema, what about that, Dad? Tell Alf about that.

Hicks: When I was a cashier at that cinema? I didn't, I didn't — oh my chest. Oh my God, I can hardly breathe. Oh God, oh God, oh. (*gasps for breath*)

(*George turns away.*)

Alf: Did 'e really fiddle the books?

Mrs Hicks: Course he didn't.

(*Pause.*)

Jay: That man coming here upsetting you all. His name will be mud in the *Daily Star*. I give you my word.

Hicks: You . . . and the *Daily Star*. Muck, that's what you are, you and the paper.

Jay: The *Daily Star* just reflects you, that's all. What you want: the glamour you'd like, the violence you'd indulge in but dare not. It's your dreams in black and white and if they seem cheap and sensational and sentimental, that's what your dreams are.

George: That's not true. It leaves out the good news. It's all slanted.

Jay: Sometimes they go wrong, we go wrong. That's natural. I'm just employed by the *Star* and not responsible for everything they put in. But I believe in what I write — true, editorially they mess around with it sometimes but . . . .

Hicks: You're vile.

Jay: The editor said, get a story about the Speaker, a personal story — nothing abstract. That's what I intended to do. What I will still do. If you read my piece you'll see that it will be a good workmanlike job.

Hicks: You used us.

Jay: You wanted to be used. You only had to say "No" right at the beginning.

Mrs Hicks: Don't argue with him.

Hicks: You and your lies about 'im liking corner houses, about 'im staying, Christ, with a humble family.

Jay: That could be true.

Hicks: Get out. You're not worth fourpence halfpenny. (*picks up suitcase and pushes it into* Jay's *arms*) Get out of my house and take that with you.

Jay: Be reasonable, Mr Hicks. Nothing is worse than before I came. (*at door*) Think it over. Everything is just the same.

(*Exit* Jay *left.*)

Hicks: Your son . . . he tried to shame me in front of Alf here and in front of that pimp of a journalist. He's a disgrace to a father.

Mrs Hicks: There, Bill.

Hicks: I don't want 'im in the house either. This is my 'ouse. I don't need any money from 'im. He can go an' live somewhere else.

Alf: Bill, Bill, c'mon now. Aw, c'mon. You'll feel different tomorrow.

Hicks: (*shouting*) Pack . . . your . . . bags.

Mrs Hicks: He didn't mean anything. He was just upset because of Sheila. Tell him you're sorry, George.

Alf: Yes, George, go on.

Mrs Hicks: (*yelling*) What are you waiting for?

(*Pause.*)

George: I'm sorry.

Hicks: That's not good enough.

Mrs Hicks: He said he was sorry.

Hicks: Tell Alf you were tellin' lies. Or else get out.

Mrs Hicks: George, please. Do as your father asks.

Alf: You've got a bad chest, Bill. He doesn't 'ave to explain that. We all know.

Hicks: Say you were tellin' lies about those jobs. Tell 'em. TELL 'EM.

Mrs Hicks: He didn't mean that. We all realise he was just saying things.

Hicks: I want to hear it from George. You tried to humiliate me. Didn't you? Tell 'em.

Alf: Words don't cost too much, George.

Mrs Hicks: Please. Please dear.

George: (*quietly*) I was telling lies.

Hicks: Say it louder. Say it louder. We hardly heard that. Loud and clear.

George: I was telling lies.

Hicks: You heard what he said, Alf?

Alf: I heard him.

Hicks: My chest feels easier, a bit easier.

Mrs Hicks: (*going over to* George, *taking his arm*) There, everything's all right.

Hicks: Yes, it's all right, George.

Alf: Course it's all right. George is a sweet-natured boy.

Hicks: It takes something to admit you're telling lies. I've got to give 'im that. There's a bit of Hicks in 'im.

Alf: You'll make it up with Sheila, George boy. Just a tiff. As the Archbishop said to the actress "Everything will look different in the morning". Tell you what. We'll make a foursome, this weekend. There's a film at the Odeon. 'The Bridge on the River Kwai'. Supposed to be good. You and Sheila and me and er, well,

I'll find a nice girl. No trouble.

Mrs Hicks: I'm sure you will, Alf.

(*Enter* Miss Chantry *from rear door right.*)

Chantry: I don't know what I said before, I was so distraught.

Mrs Hicks: We were all distraught, Betty.

Chantry: Such a headache. I fear I talked nonsense about my beloved Harry. If it wasn't for that fire . . . .

Mrs Hicks: We understand, dear.

Chantry: He was a hero and died a hero's death.

Hicks: Sure, sure.

George: As you say, Alf, it was a tiff. Sheila will change her mind tomorrow.

Mrs Hicks: Everything's all right now. Everything's back to normal.

(Alf *picks up a newspaper.*)

Hicks: Come and 'ave a game of chess, George. One before turning in.

George: All right.

Hicks: And don't knock the board over this time when I'm winning.

Alf: Mmm. See old Douglas Jardine has died.

Hicks: When I'm white I win because I am white.

George: And when I'm black I win because I am Botvinnik.

George and Hicks: Ha!

(George *and* Hicks *play chess.*)

Mrs Hicks: Who's Douglas Jardine, Alf?

Alf: Cricketer. Captain of England, he was. One of my heroes when I was a boy. Him and J.C. Clay who played for Glamorgan.

Hicks: What Jardine die of? Diphtheria? Ha ha ha. Like them tortoises, eh George?

George: (*waving piece*) There!

Alf: Know that proverb: "If the rich could hire the poor to die for them what a wonderful living the poor would make!"

Hicks: By damn, that was a good move.

Mrs Hicks: Listen, listen.

Alf: It's the van. It's back.

(George *goes over to the window, opens it.*)

Chantry: (*excited*) Yes, yes, it's the van.

Voice: (*off*) Three four five six seven. Tomorrow night at Sunshine Hall (*fainter*) One two three four . . .

Chantry: You hear that? He's going to speak tomorrow at Sunshine Hall. It's true, it's true.

Mrs Hicks: (*happily*) Yes, it's true. Jay was right. It's true, Bill.

Voice: (*off, faint*) Tomorrow at Sunshine Hall. One . . .

All join in the count: Two three four five six seven.

Alf: At Sunshine Hall.

(*They all laugh, half cheer.*)

Hicks: Close the window, Alf. My chest. It's a real arctic wind.

(*Lights down*)

THE DOGS OF PAVLOV

Characters

Sally Parsons
Kurt Jennings
Liz
S.J.Gordon
Mr Harley-Hoare
Dr Michael Daly
Dr Olwen Jones
Nurse

ACT ONE

Scene One

(*London 1968. The Chairman's Office.* S.J.Gordon, *a man in his late fifties, is peering through the window with a pair of binoculars.* Gordon *has a habit of laughing silently, making a continuous 'S' piercing sound as he does so. Now he is watching* Sally Parsons, *a young woman of 24, who is far left stage near a wall. On the wall, in whitewash, are painted the letters* WILSON EN. Sally *is adding a* D *to this incomplete slogan. Enter right,* Mr Harley-Hoare *who, observing* S.J.Gordon *observing* Sally, *coughs to draw attention to himself.*)

Gordon: (*still staring through binoculars*) What is it?
Harley-Hoare: I wonder if I could have a word with you, sir.
Gordon: I'm waiting for a call from New York. (*pause*) That woman is potty. I tell you she's potty.
Harley-Hoare: Pardon?
    (*As* Gordon *lets the binoculars drop from his eyes the spot on* Sally *fades.* Sally *now continues her slogan in the dark though*

what she writes cannot for the moment be seen by the audience.
Gordon *faces* Harley-Hoare.)
If it's not convenient I'll . . .
Gordon: Oh sit down, man.
Harley-Hoare: Thank you. I . . . er . . . .
Gordon: You want a rise. You look as if you've stomped into this office intent on asking for a rise.
Harley-Hoare: I . . . er. The prices in London, sir, are rising all the time.
Gordon: Mr Harley-Hoare, everybody wants a rise. I can't afford to employ Rockefeller as a chief clerk. You're still in the same department?
Harley-Hoare: In your nephew's. I'm with Mr Kurt Jennings, sir.
Gordon: Kurt's not my nephew. I'm his guardian. Never mind.
Harley-Hoare: I've been here since '46, sir, straight from the RAF. I have three kids, sir — one at an expensive school.
Gordon: (*going to window*) Yes, you're a solid citizen, but as for a rise at this particular time, it's not on.
Harley-Hoare: I hope I give every satisfaction.
Gordon: Come on, man. "I hope I give every satisfaction." You sound like a tart.
(Gordon, *at window, raises his binoculars and light comes up on* Sally *who has now written WILSON END VI and has started on an E.*)
Now she's a tart, a real tart.
Harley-Hoare: Perhaps, at least, I could do some overtime? Some overtime or well, well even . . . . I mean, sir, you have guinea pigs. In the laboratory, sir. I want to be a volunteer.
(Gordon *lowers binoculars. Spot down on* Sally.)
Gordon: How do you mean?
Harley-Hoare: I know we don't use human guinea-pigs in our laboratories. But I hear we have some liaison with the hospitals.
Gordon: Oh. Easy. Fine. We're financing an experiment for Dr Daly. You could be one of the subjects. Something to do with the learning process. I don't understand this one quite but they've done favours for us with our new drugs in the past so now we're being altruistic — casting our bread upon the waters. No use to the firm this particular experiment.

Harley-Hoare: It doesn't involve drugs?

Gordon: No.

Harley-Hoare: I'd be glad if you'd fix it up for me, sir. I could use some extra cash.

Gordon: Yes, there's a small fee. Something to do with statistics, I think. God knows, Dr Daly's mad on statistics.

Harley-Hoare: Well, thank you, sir. (*rises from chair*) I'm glad you can help.

Gordon: You were a pilot during the war, weren't you? A flight-sergeant or something?

Harley-Hoare: I was only 20 when the war ended. I never saw action.

Gordon: Did you want to?

Harley-Hoare: Wasn't that keen, sir. I remember once, we were out on an exercise flying over the sea and there, down on some rocks, there were masses of them.

Gordon: (*turning to watch* Sally *again with binoculars*) Masses of what?

Harley-Hoare: Seals.

(*Light up on* Sally. *On the wall now is written* WILSON END VIETN . . .)

Gordon: Seals?

Harley-Hoare: I'm boring you, sir. I'm sorry.

(Gordon *takes down binoculars. Light down on* Sally.)

Gordon: What about those seals?

Harley-Hoare: Oh, well. One of our mob banked down and started shooting them up. We all went daft, the whole lot of us, firing our guns at the seals on the rocks. That was all the action I really saw.

Gordon: And that's the end of your seal story?

Harley-Hoare: It is really — except that the seals tried to slide into the sea. Then we all saw it. The foam at the edge of the sea not white — but blood-red.

Gordon: Blood-red?

Harley-Hoare: The fringe of the sea, the disconcerting colour of raw meat.

(*Pause.*)

Gordon: What are your hobbies?

Harley-Hoare: Hobbies? Oh, I like ballroom dancing.

Gordon: *Ballroom dancing?* Christ! Well, I see. I bet you're a very dainty ballroom dancer. I used to go dancing. Ambrose, Harry Roy, Henry Hall. Before your time, eh?

Harley-Hoare: When I was a boy I . . . .

Gordon: I used to like that signature tune of Harry Roy's. (*sings*) 'She was a good girl until I took her to a dance!' Ha ha ha. Good tunes they had in those days.

Harley-Hoare: (*sings*) But why did she fall for the leader of the band?

Gordon: That's it. That's it exactly.

(*Phone rings.*)

Pick it up.

Harley-Hoare: Pardon?

Gordon: PICK IT UP.

Harley-Hoare: S.J. Gordon's office.

Gordon: New York?

Harley-Hoare: Pardon? Who? Oh, Dr Daly. Mr Gordon's right here, Dr Daly. It's Dr Daly.

Gordon: (*taking phone*) Just a minute, Dr Daly. (*to* Harley-Hoare) Come back and see me tomorrow.

Harley-Hoare: Thank you, sir.

(Harley-Hoare *begins to exit but lingers at door.*)

Gordon: Himself speaking. Ha ha ha. Nice of you to call. How's Mrs Daly? Just a moment. (*puts hand over receiver and speaks to* Harley-Hoare) Piss off, now, there's a good chap.

(*Exit* Harley-Hoare.)

The actress. Yes, Sally Parsons. Good — she's coming tomorrow? Mmm? O.K. I'll raise the ante — long as you use Sally Parsons. The experiment will last some six months, I take it? Uh huh. By the way, I have a volunteer for you. Right. Name of Harley-Hoare. Harley hyphenated Hoare. No, a normal solid citizen. No, no, sorry. I have a call coming any minute from New York. Yes. And thank *you*, Dr Daly. (*puts phone down and lights cigar then switches on intercom machine*) Theodora, is that private investigator or whatever he calls himself here yet? Good, good. Show him in, will you?

(Gordon *now goes to the window. Spot up on wall.* Sally *has now gone but her slogan remains* WILSON END VIETNAPALM. *Spot goes down on wall and on* Gordon. *Stage in Darkness. Lights on for Scene 2.*)

Scene Two

(*Next morning in the laboratory.* Dr Michael Daly *is talking to* Dr Olwen Jones. *In the background right there is a panel affair with different coloured levers, and left the 'electric chair'.*)

Daly: And I'm just haunted by it. Oh, I know, in a psychological laboratory such as ours one should try for cold objectivity — *yet* . . .

Jones: In 1945 you weren't even a doctor.

Daly: They were so short of people, you see. They were happy to accept even final year medical students, green as we were. I was aware that I wasn't volunteering for a picnic but how can one begin to imagine a Death Camp?

Jones: How terrible.

Daly: Sam Howard — one of the other students who went to Belsen — got typhus and died. I was lucky.

Jones: Then I don't see how this experiment can be anything but a personal matter for you.

Daly: It mustn't be. Yet I can't forget what happened. I can't forget what I saw. I keep thinking how somewhere still, if the register should be called, the answer would come back, "I am Auschwitz, I am Belsen, I am Buchenwald, I am Dachau."

(*Enter* Nurse *and* Sally.)

Nurse: This is Miss Parsons, Dr Daly.

Daly: Dr Gelber's patient?

Nurse: No, no, the actress. It's 11 o'clock, sir. You said to show her in at 11.

Daly: Heavens, is it as late as that already? I'm sorry Miss . . . ?

Sally: Parsons.

Daly: Would you be good enough to lay on coffee for all of us, nurse?

(*Exit* Nurse.)

Daly: It's very good of you to come to this rehearsal.

Sally: You mean audition.

Daly: Well . . . audition — but er, I understand you've been at RADA and generally had quite a lot of acting experience, Rep.

and so on.

Jones: I'm sure you'll be superb.

Sally: I gather that you are going to investigate the power of commands, evil commands.

Daly: Yes, right. What has been called the banality of Evil.

Jones: You've seen this colour chart, I think. You know how the colours go up in increments of 40 volts?

Sally: Yes, I've memorised that. White equals 40 volts.

Daly: At white you'll feel nothing.

Sally: Pink equals 80 volts, purple 120, blue 160 volts.

Daly: At pink I want you to grunt. At purple to complain verbally.

Sally: And at blue I have to ask to be released from the experiment.

Jones: Very good.

Sally: Then come the traffic lights: green, amber, and finally red. Green would be 200 volts — that's when I begin to scream, amber equals 240 and red 280.

Daly: You will really have to scream murder at 280.

Jones: If the red is pressed again and again the current is still supposed to go up in increments of 40 volts, do you understand, to a maximum of 400 volts which of course is dangerous. Very dangerous.

Sally: Surely it won't go that far?

Daly: It probably will. At Yale, the vast majority obeyed the commands no matter how insistent, how vehement the objections of the person in the so-called electric chair.

Sally: How depressing.

Daly: Shameful. And the results were validated in several other American universities also. All subjects, alas, administered shocks up to the red, very painful level. And 62 per cent went to the maximum, to the dangerous, severe shock level.

Jones: I have a sneaking hope that the ordinary Englishman with his traditions of fair play will frequently put the brake on when he comes to the traffic lights.

Daly: I doubt it. As a doctor, in the secrecy of the consulting room, haven't we listened to apparently normal, decent, English people and heard such bloody awful sadistic fantasies? In the course of a single day, after seeing the usual Smiths and

Robinsons, have we not listened to the heartbeat of an Eichmann, seen the X-ray of a Hitler, palpated the liver of Goering, read the electroencephalograph of Goebbels?

Jones: We'll see. Anyway the experiment we are going to do here is going to be different. Will you sit in our hot seat, Miss Parsons? You seem very well briefed so we should get on with our rehearsal.

(Sally *moves to chair.*)

Sally: Is this not an audition? You keep saying rehearsal. (*she sits in chair*)

Daly: I'll just clasp this round your neck. Good . . . . Mr Gordon told us himself personally your credentials, so we rang up your agent. Now your wrists please.

Sally: Mr Gordon? What has he to do with this laboratory — or for that matter, me?

Daly: Now your ankles. Thank you. The S.J. Gordon pharmaceutical company has often been generous to this laboratory. There, can you move?

(Sally *shakes her head.*)

Will you kindly pull the levers in this instance, Dr Jones?

Jones: Certainly.

Daly: We won't bother with the numbers.

Sally: What numbers?

Daly: We won't bother doing any arithmetic.

Sally: I don't follow you.

Daly: You see, normally I'll be asking for the levers to be pulled down at frequent and successive intervals — and I would continue to do this unless you add up certain sums correctly, do you understand?

Sally: If you find I'm not suitable you won't hire me simply because Mr Gordon wants you to?

Daly: Of course not. I wouldn't have this experiment ruined. If you were inept then the whole thing would be bungled, Miss er . . . ?

Sally: Fair enough. But I'm puzzled why Mr Gordon should recommend me.

Daly: It's immaterial. As I was saying, we try to let the person pulling the levers believe we are interested in hurrying up the learning process. That to him — or to her — is the object of this experiment.

Jones: Whoever pulls these levers must believe he is participating in a scientific experiment, and thereby, do you see, nobly serving the great cause of science itself. He must also believe that you really are having shocks, and must not guess you are merely acting.

Daly: Are you ready, Miss . . . Miss . . . .

Sally: I don't mind — but you do keep forgetting my name, Dr Daly.

Daly: Oh dear. You're quite right. I'm sorry.

Sally: It's Sally, Sally Parsons . . . .

Jones: She feels you're trying to depersonalise her. That she's a victim without a human name.

Daly: She's got a point. I'm sorry, very sorry, Sally. Now I'll turn down the lights if you're ready. (*he turns down the lights and shouts*) Right. Lever number one. The white lever. PULL.

(*Suddenly* Sally *is flooded with a white spotlight as* Dr Jones *pulls down white lever.*)

Jones: You don't feel anything with that.

Sally: You said white equals only 40 volts.

Jones: You could just look apprehensive.

Daly: She does look apprehensive.

Sally: Doctor . . . Please . . .

Daly: What's the matter?

Sally: I'd rather you asked me to do the sums. We may as well do this audition like a real rehearsal.

Daly: OK, add 20, 19 and 102. Now I count, OK? Add 20, 19 and 102. (*pause*) 1,2,3,4,5.

Sally: 141.

Daly: Right, 22, 108, 241. (*pause*) 1,2,3,4,5.

Sally: 371.

Daly: Right, 47, 48, 49. (*pause*) 1,2,3,4,5,6.7,8,9,10. PULL THE PINK LEVER.

(Jones *pulls the pink.* Sally *is now in pink spotlight.*)

Sally: Aaow, oooh, eeh.

Jones: That was 80 volts, wasn't it?

Daly: Yes, shall we continue? You'll see after a short interval when the current er, as it were, turns off, the light will revert to white.

Sally: Yes.

(*Enter* Nurse *with coffee.*)

Daly: 59, 104, 127. (*pause*) 1,2,3,4,5,6,7,8,9,

Sally: 294.

Daly: Wrong. PULL THE PURPLE.

(*Purple spot on* Sally *when* Dr Jones *pulls the purple lever.*)

Sally: Oh hell. That was too much. That is too much. TOO MUCH I SAY. Oh, dear, oh dear, oh dear, oh dear. STOP. Oh, oh, aah.

(*Spot reverts to white.*)

Daly: Very good, Miss Parsons.

Sally: You remember my name.

Nurse: Shall I put the lights on?

Daly: Yes, yes, good. (*lights go on*) Coffee, just what the doctor ordered.

(Dr Daly *goes over to release* Sally. Nurse *offers coffee to* Dr Jones.)

Sally: Don't you want to continue?

Daly: No, no. I can see. You'll be perfect.

Jones: No, thank you.

Nurse: Are you all right, Dr Jones?

Jones: Sorry, I just . . . just . . . .

Daly: It was only a rehearsal for heaven's sake.

Jones: Yes, of course. I'm very sorry. I'll be all right in a minute. You can easily forget the chair's not truly wired up.

Daly: Do have the coffee, Olwen. (*to* Sally) You see you were very convincing. One thing though. When we actually do our experiment could you make yourself perhaps a little less glamorous? I mean could you look older perhaps? A bit of make-up.

Jones: I'm awfully sorry, Dr Daly.

Daly: That's perfectly all right. You're better?

Jones: I do agree with you about Miss Parsons. I think if she were a little disguised the results might be more typical. Some people may be loath to bring down the levers when there's a very pretty girl in the chair.

Daly: I don't know. Some may be more willing!

Sally: I can make myself look older very easily.

Nurse: Dr Gelber phoned down to the office to ask if you'd come up to the NPC and see his patient there — when you're through here, that is.

Daly: Yes, of course. *NPC!* We have to endure that kind of vocabulary, Miss Parsons.

Sally: (*puzzled*) Pardon?

Daly: NPC. Isn't that a horrible abbreviation? It means neuro-psychiatric casualty. Then we speak of EEG of electro-encephalogram. ECG for electrocardiograph, and so on. Yes, we abbreviate everything because our terms are so unspeakable. Right down to BID.

Sally: BID?

Jones: Brought in Dead.

Sally: Oh . . . . That was my first part in rep!

Daly: Tell Dr Gelber we'll be up very shortly.

Nurse: Yes, I will, sir.

(*Exit* Nurse.)

Daly: And we'll see you tomorrow at 10, Miss Parsons. Meanwhile, not a word to anyone about the nature of the experiment. It would spoil things if, outside these walls, it became known that we hired an actress.

Sally: Then I am hired?

Daly: Of course. We'll take you on for a week and if you're satisfactory, as I'm sure you will be, we will arrange a six months' contract.

Sally: Thank you. Thank you both.

(*Exit* Sally.)

Daly: She'll be fine.

Jones: So good she made me feel a little faint.

Daly: You're a softie, Olwen.

(*Pause.*)

Jones: I heard the roll call you mentioned: "I am Auschwitz, I am Belsen, I am Buchenwald." I pulled fake levers and stupidly I heard ghosts scream. (Dr Jones *pulls down red lever and red light floods the electric chair*) I think I became a doctor because I wanted to relieve suffering. Yet other people's suffering is the one thing I still find most hard to bear. All through my medical career, I have had this central problem. You're right. I'm soft, soft, soft. What an idiot I am.

Daly: (*putting hand sympathetically on her shoulder*) Well, don't worry, Olwen. The suffering we'll witness in this laboratory will be only a pretence (*looking at his watch*). We'd better see Gelber's patient.

Jones: You probably know those lines of Yeats: "I must lie down where all the ladders start, In the foul rag-and-bone shop of the heart."

Daly: My wife was telling me what James Joyce took for his motto: Satan's "Non Serviam," I will not obey.

(*Exit Daly and* Jones. *Lights go down leaving only red spot on the 'electric chair' which fades gradually to darkness.*)

Scene Three

(*It is late.* Kurt's *rather luxurious flat is softly lit.* Kurt, *a blond young man, is sitting on a sofa with* Sally *who has a glass in her hand and who, in fact, is slightly drunk. They are listening to some music on the record player. Very soon the music, a Beethoven quartet, concludes and the record player automatically clicks as the record lifts off.*)

Sally: What time ish it?

Kurt: Time for bed. Also time you stopped drinking. (*he takes the glass from her hand*) What time ish it? You can't even pronounce your s's.

Sally: I can. She sells seashells on the sea shore. She sells seashells on the seashore.

Kurt: It's nearly midnight, Sally.

Sally: I think you're a sex maniac. (*pause*) Thank God.

(Kurt *takes the record off and puts it away.*)

Kurt: I agree with you. I should be in the *Who's Who of Sex Maniacs*. And you're a chatterbox and more than a bit sloshed.

Sally: (*grumbling*) You always agree with me. For the whole month I've known you, you haven't had the British decency to quarrel with me. Even when I talk politics you just smile. Right?

Kurt: Right.

Sally: (*tearful*) You're never serious with me, Kurt. Never really serious. I'm older than you but you treat me like a naughty kid. You never confide in me. I tell you everything about myself, absolutely everything.

Kurt: You haven't even told me about your mysterious audition this morning.

97

Sally: Don't try to change the subject. Nobody's ever called me reticent. But you are. You're so secretive. Besides, you only listen to half of what I say.

Kurt: Less than that.

Sally: You don't! Before I put on that record, what did I say, go on what did I bloody well say?

Kurt: As a matter of fact you read me that bit from the *Evening Standard*. About John Allison being a smash hit in that Broadway show. You were trying to needle yourself.

Sally: No, no, sorry. Before that, I mean.

Kurt: Do you mean about how you dried up in some play you were in at Bath?

Sally: It was a first night in bloody Lincoln. There you are!

Kurt: You said bloody Bath.

Sally: Lincoln definitely. Lincoln's *miles* away from Bath. Kurt, could we go to the theatre tomorrow night?

Kurt: What's on?

(Sally *picks up the* Evening Standard.)

Kurt: I must say most theatre people are a pain in the neck. Especially the men.

Sally: Thank you! Thank you for that.

Kurt: Well, every actor I've ever met at a party has one eye on the person he's talking to and the other on the rest of the company to see what sort of impression he's making. Except of course poor Freddie Gee.

Sally: Poor Freddie Gee?

Kurt: Yes, he only had one eye.

(Sally *throws cushion at* Kurt *who catches it. They smile at each other. The front doorbell rings.*)

Who the devil?

(Kurt *looks out of the window.* Sally *helps herself to more whisky.*)

That's Gordon's new car. What can *he* want *now*?

Sally: New car?

Kurt: Yes, he's got another Daimler. He changes his car every time the ashtrays get full. I'd better let him in.

(Kurt *takes glass off* Sally *just as she's about to drink from it. He waves a castigating finger at her, drinks it up himself and makes for the door.*)

Sally: Kurt.

Kurt: Mmmm?

Sally: Funny, you being a sales director. I mean in a pharmaceutical firm! Christ!

Kurt: You see me more as an astronaut or a professional tennis player perhaps?

(Sally *shakes her head. Exit* Kurt. Sally *picks up the paper. Reads out:* Charlie Girl; The Mousetrap; Fiddler on the Roof; Canterbury Tales; Hair; Lock up Your Daughters. *Enter* Gordon *and* Kurt.)

Gordon: Sorry to barge in like this. I didn't realise . . . I know! You must be the girl who used to be friendly with Allison, John Allison.

Kurt: I never told you that.

Gordon: You must have done. Some people think I'm a wizard but I haven't got psychic powers.

Sally: It doesn't matter. It's not a secret.

Gordon: He's doing well on Broadway, isn't he?

Kurt: Gordon, you haven't come round to talk about Broadway stars at this hour.

Gordon: You're sharp with me, Kurt. Shall I come back tomorrow? I have good news for you though.

Kurt: Well?

Gordon: It's really very exciting news. (*he lights a cigarette- then to* Sally) Oh, sorry, cigarette?

Kurt: C'mon, Gordon. Stop teasing me.

Gordon: (*laughs noiselessly*) Ha ha ha.

Kurt: Ever since I was so high he's enjoyed teasing me.

Gordon: And he was such a lovely, handsome kid to tease. Really, when I walked down the street with him people turned their heads.

Sally: He's not so bad now.

Gordon: (*smiling*) He's gone off a bit. At least he's going off month by month. Definitely. Blondes lose their looks quickly. Their mouths get slack. They get flushed in the face. They get fat. I know. I married one. Their menopause comes on quick; their teeth come out quicker than darker people like me. I'm 58 and I have all my teeth. What do you think of that? Every single tooth in my head is my own.

Sally: Your dentist must be very proud of you.

Gordon: Ha ha ha.

Kurt: Gordon, what's this great news?

Gordon: Make me some coffee, Kurt, be hospitable. Then I'll tell you why I've come.

Kurt: Have a Scotch.

Gordon: (*sternly*) Coffee.

Sally: I'll make you some . . .

Gordon: No, Kurt — Kurt you make it.

> (Kurt *hesitates. There is a short tense pause.*)

I said I'd like some coffee, Kurt.

Kurt: Sure, of course.

Gordon: (*soundlessly*) Ha ha ha.

> (*Exit* Kurt.)

Sally: What's the good news you have for Kurt, Mr Gordon?

Gordon: Please don't call me, Mr Gordon. Everybody calls me Gordon. Even my wife. My first name, you see, is impossible.

Sally: Is it Clarence?

Gordon: No, no.

Sally: Marmaduke

> (Gordon *shakes his head.*)

Elias?

> (Gordan *shakes his head again.*)

Buster! It's that — Buster!

Gordon: (*laughing noiselessly*) Ha ha ha. No, you'll never guess. Anyway nobody's called me it for a long time. For a while people called me Flash Gordon. But I loathed that. When you're as colourful a character as I am it's too near the gums to be called Flash. Now you're a colourful character, too, Miss Parsons.

Sally: Thank you.

Gordon: Artists, artistes. Funny people. Oh, I'm eccentric, people think me odd, but I've got my feet on the ground. I don't go scrawling on walls.

Sally: What do you mean?

Gordon: (*loud*) I don't go scrawling on walls. (*quieter*) Artists. They're up there. Take drugs some of them, hit the bottle. You like a drop, I know that.

Sally: Well, I . . . .

Gordon: Slash their wrists, some of them, even. Ha ha ha. Well, mental pain is very real. Real as physical pain so the psychiatrists say. And Kurt could bear witness to that.

Sally: How do you mean?

Gordon: He's a nervy boy.

Sally: I wouldn't say that. Kurt seems very normal and stable to me.

Gordon: You're wrong. To have had a German father who was a prisoner-of-war and an English mother who died when he was only twelve years old, you think that's a good start in life?

Sally: He overcame. You helped him. When he went to boarding school —

Gordon: HEIL HITLER! (*pause*) That was his father's suicide note. That's all Kurt's father left behind him. Two words on a scrap of paper. Is it any wonder Kurt took his mother's surname?

Sally: I don't know what you're trying to tell me.

Gordon: Kurt is 22.

Sally: So?

Gordon: I look around. I see young men of 22 carefree, in jeans, in sweaters, not acting ten years older than they are — like Kurt. It's a disguise. Kurt's coiled up. He could crack again.

Sally: Again? Why do you say "again"?

Gordon: Kurt needs somebody very responsible. Sober, sensible, somebody with a low emotional temperature.

Sally: What right? Holy Lenin, what right? I mean you don't know me. I don't know what judgements you're making or what assumptions you're basing your judgement on.

Gordon: Pain, pain's a terrible thing — physical or mental. Otherwise it would be a sweet world.

(*Enter* Kurt *with coffee.*)

Kurt: Sweet world? Sometimes it is, yes.

Gordon: I was just telling Miss Parsons what it takes to make a sweet world. I was saying how I dream that one day our pharmaceutical company will discover a new marvellous analgesic, some wonderful pain killer.

Sally: You weren't talking about any . . . .

Gordon: (*loud*) Kurt, I just came round to tell you you're off to New York.

Kurt: New York?

Gordon: You've got the job. David Quinn's retiring. You're taking the whole American office over, Kurt.

Kurt: Why Gordon, that's . . . that's fantastic. Sal, you don't know. When, Gordon?

Gordon: 'Bout a month, I guess. By the time I fix things up properly. Thought you'd like a month's grace. Course you can go out sooner. (*looking at* Sally) Maybe it would be best to go out sooner and get some overlap with David.

(Gordon *goes up to* Kurt. *Takes his arm gently. They look at each other with great concentration.*)

(*gently*) It's what you want, isn't it?

Kurt: You know.

(Gordon *slowly raises his right hand to* Kurt's *left chest and lets it lie there.* Gordon *looks at* Sally.)

Gordon: Good boy. Good . . . boy. (*takes his hand away*) Well that's it then.

(Kurt *takes* Gordon's *hand and kisses it briefly.*)

(*soundlessly*) Ha ha ha. I wanted to tell you tonight. As soon as I heard Quinn's decision. I wanted to see your face, see you happy. I'm so sorry. I didn't know you weren't alone or I'd have waited till the morning.

(Gordon *begins to exit*)

Sally: Mr Gordon, I still don't understand.

Gordon: I'll see myself out.

Sally: What about your coffee?

Gordon: At this time of night? It would keep me awake. Even without it, I'll sleep the sleep of fever.

Kurt: Thank you, Gordon.

Gordon: I'm glad your audition worked out, Miss Parsons.

Sally: It did work out, yes.

Gordon: Good, good.

(*Exit* Gordon.)

Kurt: It's marvellous. It really is.

Sally: Why should Gordon help me with that audition?

Kurt: What? Tell me about this audition. What's the play? Where is it? Must you keep it a secret?

Sally: I don't like Gordon. I don't like that man.

Kurt: I'd like you to like him. He loves me in his own way. Like a favourite uncle.

Sally: He touched you on the chest, Kurt.

Kurt: What?

Sally: As if you were a woman. Sexually, I mean.

Kurt: What are you talking about? For heaven's sake, Sally.

Sally: He said he loved you.

Kurt: Like an uncle I said. You know I have no parents. You know he was a friend of my mother.

Sally: Does he say he loves you?

Kurt: You must stop this.

Sally: All right! Not in the way I mean. In the way you mean — does he say he loves you?

Kurt: I'm a bit old for him to say that to me now.

(*Pause.*)

Sally: Do you remember your father at all?

Kurt: Not really, not much. Funny, when I do think of him, one image keeps coming back. He'd taken three lemons from a bowl on the sideboard. It's really my first memory. I was just an infant.

Sally: Three lemons?

Kurt: Yes, and he's juggling them. To amuse me. He's throwing up high, one two three lemons, and he's shouting excitedly, "Look, look, look." And I'm looking. There's a window to the left and there's my father near the sideboard, his mouth open as he juggles the three lemons. He appears to be utterly happy.

Sally: Is this a dream?

Kurt: No, it's true! I think it's true. My father's face is uplifted and lit up from within, and he's juggling and the three lemons don't fall to the carpet when he steps forward, nor when he steps backward, shouting, "Look Kurt!" I find it so hard to believe he killed himself. I think of him juggling lemons and happy. (*pause*) Sally, listen, this job. Do you know what goes with it? For a start there's 50,000 dollars a year. *Fifty thousand.* Then there's the so-called ancillary benefits. There's expenses and the apartment near Washington Square. You should see that apartment, like a penthouse. Right up high, it overlooks — you should see. You *will* see. On one side the Hudson River; on the other, the East River. You can see the big liners coming slowly in.

Sally: Sounds like a dream or a film shot. It's just not *real*. You make New York sound idyllic. It isn't. It's on the road to hell. I doubt if you'll ever see a rainbow in the sky over New York. One day a dove will drown on the top of the Empire State

Building.

Kurt: Sally, before you get on to me again about the colour problem or Vietnam or whatever, listen . . . *listen.* I want you to come with me. Come live with me in New York.

Sally: And be your love.

Kurt: Sure. *I'm serious.* (*pause*) I'm asking you to marry me. (*Long pause.*) Well, what do you say, chatterbox?

Sally: Marry?

Kurt: That's right.

Sally: I don't understand. I've been drinking, not you.

Kurt: You want me to be old-fashioned? Go down on my knees?

Sally: But Kurt, we don't know . . . .

Kurt: Each other? We *do.*

Sally: In the Biblical sense, yes. It's just . . . just . . . .

Kurt: Just what? Just what what what?

Sally: Just that there are a few notes missing on the piano keyboard, know what I mean?

Kurt: Frankly, no.

Sally: Just, just that there's no sound here and there and I don't know what music it is I'm not hearing. I'm scared of that. On the top key, the sound of felt.

Kurt: The sound of felt?

Sally: It's a big decision. *For both of us.* Besides, Gordon doesn't like me.

Kurt: Gordon's not asking you. *I am.*

(*Suddenly* Sally *puts her hands over her face.*)

I've never asked anyone before. (*jokingly*) This is a hell of a reception. (*decisively*) Let's talk about it in bed. (*pause*) Sally. What's the matter?

(*She keeps her hands over her face and* Kurt *goes over to her. He brings up his hands to touch her head gently, but hesitates.*)

Sally. Please. Don't . . . .

(*Lights down.*)

Scene Four

(*Right stage,* Liz, *a young woman, is standing on the top of a rubbish bin and is writing a slogan on the wall. So far she has written STOP YANKEE . . . . Near her, looking right and left, is* Sally. *Left stage, a room in* Gordon's *apartment.* Gordon, *who is alone, is putting a tape on a recorder.*)

Liz: My arm's getting tired.
Sally: All right, let me finish it.
Liz: I'll just do one m-m-m-more word. How m-m-many walls are we going to do tonight?
Sally: This'll be the last.
Liz: M-m-my God. I don't know if it does any good. I m-m-m-mean what about the b-b-ber-back-lash?
Sally: Aw, Liz, come down. I'll finish it.
Liz: Last year it was B-B-Ber-Biafra. Or Enoch Powell. Besides this place is a b-b-ber-back alley. Nobody comes here. Only one space-man every leap year will see this slogan.
Sally: It may not do any good. But it makes me feel better.
Liz: I don't feel any b-b-better.
Sally: All right, go home. I'm not stopping you.
Liz: I'll do just one m-m-more word.
(Liz *begins to paint on the wall the word BUTCHERS. Meanwhile,* Sally *lights a cigarette and the tape comes on. Then* Gordon *sits down listening to it.*)
Man's Voice: From Brixton to the fleshpots is fine. West Indian boy brought up in Brixton is fine. The early struggles and the gangs are fine. But what about Sally Parsons? My paper would be interested in that.
Allison: I'd rather we left Sally out of it.
Man: Well, tell me off the record.
(*The front doorbell of* Gordon's *apartment now rings.*)
Allison: But this is being taped.
Man: I give you my word. Nothing in the whole article — including stuff about Sally Parsons — will be used without your personal OK.
(*Bell goes again.* Gordon *knocks tape recorder off. Then he exits.*)

Liz: Some people would think it very adolescent Sal, putting slogans on walls. A b-b-bit daft.

Sally: You're getting so . . . middle class. Come down and let me finish it.

Liz: M-my God. I *am* m-m-m-middle class. (*she jumps down off the bin*) We'll get picked up by the police one night I b-b-b-bet you. That fella keeping an eye on us the other evening was a policeman probably. Let's pack it in.

Sally: Give me the brush.

Liz: Why is it so important to you?

(*Pause.*)

Sally: I don't know. (*pause*) Go home. You go home.

Liz: Can't go home. Well I can, only Dad's in a stinking temper — like a m-m-mad bear. Like Stalin.

Sally: Are you going to give me the brush?

Liz: Just one team let him down this week in the football pools. It's m-m-made him m-m-mad.

Sally: Football pools?

Liz: Wish that team had drawn. Would have won thousands. (*gives* Sally *the brush*) Just one team. B-B-Ber. Oh dear. Ber-Ber-Ber.

Sally: Give me a hand up.

Liz: Ber-Ber-Ber.

Sally: Birmingham?

Liz: No, er B-B-Ber.

Sally: Bristol City?

(*Liz shakes her head.*)

Bristol Rovers?

Liz: No. Ber-

Sally: Burnley.

Liz: Ber-Ber-

Sally: Brighton?

Liz: No. B-B-B-Ber-Ber-Bloody Aston Villa. (*pause*) What are you smiling at? If Aston Villa had drawn the whole quality of my life would have changed.

Sally: I suppose I could change the quality of my life by getting married.

Liz: Definitely. Wonder if it's worth putting an ad in the paper. Excellent typist, white liberal, very fast rate, can provide home for handsome m-m-m-millionaire.

Sally: Somebody has asked me to marry him.

Liz: Rich?

Sally: Yes.

Liz: M-my God. Lucky dab.

Sally: I don't know.

Liz: You still in love with John?

(Sally *shakes her head. Enter stage left,* Kurt *and* Gordon.)

Liz: Wish someone would ber-ber-ber-bloody ask me.

Sally: What happened to that Yank who was chasing you?

Liz: Well, I said you can't lay your hands on m-m-m-me until you take your hands off Vietnam.

(Sally *climbs onto the bin and continues the slogan on the wall.*)

Gordon: I can't pretend not to be disturbed.

Kurt: I thought you'd be delighted.

Gordon: It's your life, your business, but I want the best for you. You know I — let me be frank — well one day — I just can't see Sally Parsons as the Empress of all *this*.

Kurt: You hardly know her.

Gordon: I know she drinks too much. I know she's been sleeping around for years. I know she used to be a communist — I know other things too.

Kurt: What do you mean, "sleeping around for years"?

Gordon: She's more experienced than Farouk was at her age. Listen, Kurt, think about it. Don't rush things. Don't you remember what's-her-name, er . . . Frances Do-dah. Wasn't I right then?

Kurt: I was just a kid.

Gordon: She was old enough to be your mother.

Kurt: She was as innocent as I was.

Gordon: At least she didn't go round like this Sally Parsons scrawling on walls, for God's sake. A woman who shacked up with that nigger actor, John Allison. (*louder*) Allison is rubbish. *Rubbish.* I've checked up on him, and he . . . .

Kurt: (*loud*) What's all this to do with Sally?

Gordon: A woman who writes on walls, *Enoch Powell is an Albino.* Jesus!

Kurt: You don't like the idea that she was a close friend of a coloured fellow. Is that it? You . . . you . . . .

(Kurt's *face is contorted.* Gordon *puts his head in his hands.*

Kurt *lights a cigarette. There is a long pause.)*
Kurt: What's the matter?
Gordon: I just got a headache.
Kurt: If you knew Sally, really knew her . . . .
Gordon: It's suddenly come on.
Kurt: Take an aspirin, take an anadin, or take one of our own products. (*He fishes in his pocket, finds a bottle of tablets and offers it to Gordon.*)
Gordon: Just a lousy headache.
Kurt: You know the ad. Nothing works faster than an anadin.
Gordon: That's why I'd rather take *nothing*!
Kurt: I better go.
Gordon: I feel responsible, Kurt. If I hadn't fixed the New York . . . if I put the kibosh on the job, what then?
Kurt: It would make no odds. Gordon, you once said to me that if things were inevitable one had to smile and accept it. You said, if it's inevitable that you're going to be raped you may as well relax and enjoy it.
Gordon: I said that?
Kurt: Yes.
Gordon: (*laughs noiselessly*) I wasn't being original. (*pause*) Kurt, I asked you to drop in tonight because I have a tape I want you to hear.
Kurt: Besides, Sally hasn't definitely said, 'yes' yet.
Gordon: She will. A girl like that, she will.
Kurt: I think you just don't want me to marry anyone.
Gordon: Everybody says silly things sometimes, but why do you have to say them deliberately? This tape, Kurt, it's a nice little talk by John Allison.
Kurt: Allison? You've got a tape of him? Sally's right. She said there's a streak of coarseness in you.
Gordon: Well, Kurt, who better than her to recognise it? Ha ha ha. Now listen to this tape.
Kurt: I'm going, Gordon. See you.
Gordon: Wait a minute, wait a second. I got that job in New York for you because I hoped that would separate you. I was worried that . . . .

(*Exit* Kurt. Gordon *goes after him.*)
Now, hang on, Kurt.

(*Right stage* Sally *has just finished the slogan:* STOP

YANKEE BUTCHERS NOW and is getting down from the bin.)

Liz: That's that. Can we go now?

(Liz *takes a bar of chocolate out of bag and offers some to* Sally.)

Sally: I'd like you to meet Kurt, Liz.

Liz: Kurt? Is that his name. My father doesn't like Huns. Now if I wrote on walls kill off every Hun he'd take off his ber-ber-bowler hat and cheer. *(pause)* Tell you what, both of you come to dinner tomorrow night. Dad will be out. Then I'll give your boy friend the once over. My valuable opinion.

Sally: OK. Somebody who knows him well tells me he's neurotic, all curled up, nervous.

Liz: Is he?

Sally: No. Not at all. But then the same person thinks I'm neurotic.

Liz: You are. I m-m-m-mean you're a 24-year-old adolescent. All adolescents are neurotic. Young people are neurotic, then they become normal for about six months — and after that they become neurotic again. I'm going through the normal stage at the moment.

Sally: Come on, let's go.

Liz: First people have no character, then they become characters and then when they become really old they become caricatures.

Sally: So sayeth the Prophet. I'm not neurotic.

Liz: You eat funny.

Sally: *(stops chewing)* What?

Liz: The way you eat. Your jaws — when you m-m-m-munch.

Sally: What?

Liz: They go side to side obliquely.

Sally: *(beginning to exit)* Really?

Liz: You have a funny way of m-m-m-masticating

(*As* Sally *and* Liz *exit, enter* Gordon *right stage. He goes over to the tape and plays it.)*

Allison: So they are junkies and queers and drunks. But so what? You don't know the heat of a New York summer.

Man: To get back to Sally Parsons. What happened when you told her it was finished?

Allison: She took it all calmly. But two hours later she was

boozed to the eyebrows and hysterical and . . . (*voice trails off*)
Man: And what?
Allison: The same day she tried to slash her wrists with a razor
blade in the bathroom. My God. She was only 23. It wasn't the
first time she tried. When she was 17 she was taken to Charing
Cross Hospital after an overdose of aspirins. Of course that was
before I knew her. I bet she still is a suicide risk.
Man: How do you feel about Sally Parsons now?
Allison: I don't feel anything. Just another white girl I knew in
the old days. It's nothing to do with my attitudes about Black
Power. There's no time for human affection any more.
(Gordon *knocks off recorder, looks pensive and lights fade.*)
Gordon: No time for human affection any more, baby.

Scene Five

(*The Laboratory. As the lights go up enter* Dr Daly *and* Dr
Jones.)

Jones: I'm afraid Sally's very frank opinions offend her, do you
see.
Daly: Well, it can't be helped. It's easier to get another nurse
at this stage of the game than another actress. By the way,
Olwen, will you manage to come to my lecture on the 28th?
Jones: If I can, yes. It's at 7p.m., isn't it? I must say you've
given it a snappy title, 'Evil Commands and Scientific
Research'; that should grab even the least active members of
the Society.
Daly: Think so?
(*Enter* Sally, *made up, looking much older.*)
Heavens, is that you, Sally?
Sally: I didn't like the other wig.
Jones: Terrific. I would never have recognised you.
Sally: Perhaps people will be less willing to electrocute me in
this wig.
Daly: Sally, there's one thing I think I ought to say. You seem
to loathe all the 25 people we've had so far in a very personal
way. You take everything so personally.

Sally: They don't know I'm acting. They think I'm a real victim. And afterwards I feel like a victim and I hate their guts.

Jones: You shouldn't allow yourself to get that involved.

Sally: What gets me is how they depreciate my worth afterwards. They say I'm stupid — that I deserve to be shocked.

Daly: The victim always has to be thought inferior. That was but one finding in other scientific experiments.

Jones: Anyway, one knows that from history.

Sally: I scream like hell and they just continue to bring down the blasted levers. Like soldiers, like bomber pilots in Vietnam, like concentration camp guards, they just do their work like a duty, and don't seem to question the basic moral premise of what they're doing. They just take pride in doing a good technical job. They're proud of their technical efficiency.

Daly: When people feel they are serving some higher cause — in this case, scientific enquiry — then consciences become startlingly soluble.

Jones: But some do want to opt out — some make verbal objections or think in their own minds, 'This is wrong' — and having made this inner protest they carry on, with their own consciences crystal clear.

Sally: A fat lot of good that does.

(*Enter* Nurse.)

Nurse: Mr Harley-Hoare is ready when you are, sir.

Daly: It's all been explained to him?

Nurse: He signed all the necessary papers and . . . .

(*Looks at* Sally *astonished.*)

Jones: Aye, it's a tidy disguise, isn't it?

Nurse: By the way, Dr Daly, my relief, Gloria Adams — Nurse Adams — will be coming next week. (*pause*) I think you knew I was going to ask for a transfer, Dr Jones.

Daly: We'll be sorry to lose you, Nurse.

Sally: It's me, isn't it?

Nurse: I'll show in Mr Harley-Hoare. (*turns to exit*)

Sally: You object to my attitudes. You think Enoch Powell . . .

Nurse: (*turning fiercely to face* Sally) . . . is refreshingly honest. I have nothing against coloured people. I'm not a racialist as you said I was yesterday. Only they *do* have a different background from us, a different culture.

Sally: I don't know how you can breathe the same air as us, nurse. You should live in a glasshouse, and people who live in glasshouses, as you know, *ought to be stoned.*

Daly: Sally!

Sally: I thought she was a nice, quiet, dull girl.

Nurse: There's no need to be impertinent.

Daly: I think you owe her an apology, Sally.

Sally: You should have learnt that it's better to remain quiet and be thought a bit dull than to talk and remove all doubt.

Nurse: (*disdainfully*) You will all be pleased to learn that my relief, Nurse Adams, is a West Indian.

(Nurse *begins to exit.*)

Daly: Just a minute. This is a scientific laboratory. Do you both understand that? And I don't want any more of these emotional blow-ups.

(*Exit* Nurse.)

Jones: Better get you ready, Sally.

Sally: I suppose so. Now for the next sweet, reasonable *human being.*

(Sally *goes to the chair and* Dr Jones *straps her in.*)

Daly: I'm sorry, but however strongly you feel I can't allow any more exhibitions of personal malice and . . .

Sally: I hear angels and church music.

Daly: Sally, I . . .

Nurse: (*off*) In there, Mr Harley-Hoare.

(*Enter* Harley-Hoare.)

Harley-Hoare: Good morning. Lovely morning.

Jones: It is, it is.

Harley-Hoare: For this time of the year, I mean.

Jones: It's all been explained to you — our little experiment?

Harley-Hoare: Yes, Dr Daly.

Jones: No, no. This is Dr Daly.

Harley-Hoare: Ah, quite. And this is the volunteer. Yes, well, shall we press on? These I take it are the levers.

Jones: You understand the purpose of the experiment.

Harley-Hoare: Just tell me what to do and I'll do it.

Sally: Oh.

Harley-Hoare: (*smiles at* Sally) Trust me.

(Sally *smiles at him.*)

Daly: Well, if you'll excuse me.

Harley-Hoare: Aren't you staying?

Daly: No, no. I've devised the experiment. I am biased in its favour. If I pulled down the levers or Dr Jones here, did that, it might hasten the learning process, which is of course what we want — but scientifically speaking it wouldn't be correct. The relationship between you and our other volunteer here must be more anonymous.

Harley-Hoare: Quite . . . er . . . quite. Yes, I see. (*pause*) I don't really understand. It's all scientific double-dutch to me. But . . . er . . . whatever you say, *doctor*, goes.

Sally: You have implicit faith in doctors?

Harley-Hoare: Where would we be without them? Ha ha ha.

Daly: I'll see you later.

(*Exit* Daly.)

Jones: Shall we begin then?

Harley-Hoare: Nurse said I am to begin with the white lever.

Jones; Exactly — then you just go along the row when she makes mistakes.

(*Lights go down.*)

Harley-Hoare: (*jovially*) Now don't make too many mistakes, my dear, will you?

(Sally *smiles.*)

Good.

(*Immediately* Harley-Hoare *pulls down a white lever and* Sally, *no longer smiling, is flooded with white spotlight.*)

Jones: Wait, wait. You musn't shock her when she hasn't made any mistakes.

Harley-Hoare: Oh sorry, sorry. I've bungled it already. Damn. Shall I knock the lever back then?

Jones: No, no. She just had a small shock, just 40 volts.

Harley-Hoare: 40 volts, yes, it goes up in increments of 40 volts as nurse told me.

Jones: Are you ready for the numbers?

Sally: Yes.

Jones: Add 20, 21, 22. (*pause*) 1,2,3.

Sally: 63.

Jones: Right. 33, 34, 35. (*pause*) 1,2,3,4.

Sally: 102.

Jones: Right.

Harley-Hoare: Very good, excellent.

Jones: 46, 47, 48. (*pause*) 1,2,3,4,5,6,7,8,9.

(Harley-Hoare *pulls pink lever.* Sally *now in pink light.* Sally *grunts.*)

You must give her a chance. I didn't count to 10. You must allow her the full ten seconds.

Harley-Hoare: Oh dear. Very, very sorry, doctor . . . . I fear I am not quite with it.

(*Pink light has faded and is replaced by white spotlight.*)

Jones: 59, 60, 61. (*pause*) 1,2,3,4,5,6,7,8.

Sally: 180.

Jones: 72, 77, 79. (*pause*) 1,2,3,4,5,6,7,8,9,10. PULL THE PURPLE.

(Harley-Hoare *pulls the purple lever and purple spot comes on* Sally.)

Sally: Oh hell, that's too much. TOO MUCH. Oh dear, oh dear, oh dear, oh . . . ah . . .

Harley-Hoare: That was OK, wasn't it? I did do that right.

Jones: Yes, quite right.

Harley-Hoare: I'm getting the hang of it, but . . . er, I'm worried about her.

Jones: 80, 84, 86. (*pause*) 1,2.

Sally: 250.

Jones: 97, 98, 104. (*pause*) 1,2,3,4,5,6,7,8,9,10. PULL THE . . . .

(Harley-Hoare *pulls the blue lever and blue light bathes* Sally's *distorted face.*)

Sally: Aw, aw, aw, aw, STOP. Please, please. Stop, stop. Oh dear, oh dear. No. Aaah.

(*Blue light begins to fade and* Sally, *in chair, closes her eyes and breathes heavily.*)

Harley-Hoare: That was quite a shock. Are you all right?

Jones: It was 160 volts.

Harley-Hoare: 160. Shall I go on?

Jones: Yes, yes. The experiment must continue.

Sally: I think I can go on.

Harley-Hoare: Fine, good.

Sally: It was very powerful though. I don't think I'd like much more.

Harley-Hoare: You must add up properly.

Sally: I'll do my best. Can I have a drink?

Jones: Are you ready, Mr Harley-Hoare?

Harley-Hoare: Yes, yes.

Sally: I'd like a drink first.

(Harley-Hoare *is now sweating and becomes more agitated as the scene continues.*)

Harley-Hoare: Can she have a drink?

Jones: We must continue without all these interruptions.

Harley-Hoare: You hear what the doctor says.

Jones: Are you ready?

Harley-Hoare: *I'm* ready.

Jones: 114, 117, 121. (*pause*) 1,2,3,4,5,6,7,8,9,10. PULL THE GREEN.

(Harley-Hoare *pulls the lever and green light floods* Sally.)

Sally: Aaah, aah, aah,aah. Pler, pler, pler, please. No no no no nono. STOP IT. YOU STOP IT. YOU BAS aw . . .

(*Light begins to fade, and again* Sally *is slumped on chair, eyes closed. White spot on.*)

Harley-Hoare: You stupid . . . . You're stupid.

Sally: Release me, please.

Harley-Hoare: What?

Sally: That was too much. Release me.

Harley-Hoare: You should add up properly.

Sally: I insist you release me.

Jones: Are you ready, Mr Harley-Hoare?

Harley-Hoare: She wants to be released.

Sally: I can't go on.

Harley-Hoare: Don't you think you ought to try? I mean we've entered into a bargain. We should honour that.

Sally: I can't take any more, I'm telling you. I just can't take it.

Harley-Hoare: What do we do, doctor?

Jones: Of course we go on.

Sally: No, I refuse. I have my rights and I refuse.

Harley-Hoare: Do what the doctor says.

Jones: 114, 118.

Sally: No, no,no. I can't add up. I can't think. Release me.

Harley-Hoare: She won't add up.

Jones: We must continue with our experiment. These experiments are important.

Harley-Hoare: I understand.

Sally: Don't pull the lever.

Jones: You must.

Harley-Hoare: I must, yes. Try and co-operate.

Sally: Don't pull it I say. The next one's a helluva big shock.

Harley-Hoare: I'm ready doctor.

Jones: 114, 118, 132. (*pause*) 1,2,3,4.

Sally: No, no.

Jones: 5,6,7,8,9.

Sally: No.

Jones: 10. PULL THE AMBER. (*the amber spot*)

Sally: Bastard bastard, bastard, bastard, BASTAARD.

Harley-Hoare: Don't swear at me. You idiot. You stupid idiot. (*pause*) Is she all right?

Jones: She will be in a sec.

Harley-Hoare: How many volts was that, doctor?

Jones: 240 volts.

Harley-Hoare: Perhaps she ought to have a drink.

Jones: Do you insist?

Harley-Hoare: I don't insist, of course not. But don't you think?

Jones: I think we should proceed.

Harley-Hoare: Well, of course, you know best. You know what you're doing . . . but she does seem exhausted.

Jones: Ah, she's recovering, do you see?

Harley-Hoare: Yes, yes.

Sally: Dr . . . Dr Jones. I can't. I CAN'T.

Harley-Hoare: Perhaps we ought to allow her to rest, but of course whatever *you* say, doctor.

Jones: I can only repeat we must continue with the experiment. The whole point is to teach her that she will get an increasing shock if she does not concentrate and add up more quickly.

Harley-Hoare: Like Pavlov's dog. We're conditioning you.

Sally: I'm not a dog.

Harley-Hoare: It does seem excruciatingly painful.

Sally: Release me, please.

Jones: If it wasn't painful, we could not hope to speed up the learning process.

Harley-Hoare: Very well. Just one more lever. This is the last, isn't it? (*to* Sally) It's the last one.

Jones: Well, by pulling the red lever back and fore, back and fore, we can go higher than 280 volts. We can go to a maximum of 400 volts.

Harley-Hoare: Wouldn't that be dangerous?

Jones: Ye-es. But the next one — 280 volts — is very high. A very bad shock.

Harley-Hoare: I don't think we should go above that. Are you all right?

Sally: No, I'm not all right. I insist you let me go. I can't bear any more.

Harley-Hoare: You shouldn't have volunteered if you can't co-operate. Out of courtesy.

Sally: Out of courtesy?

Harley-Hoare: I'm committed.

Jones: 799, 899, 999. Add up.

Sally: Don't. Don't. I beg you.

Harley-Hoare: You must speak to the doctor, not to me. I'm just obeying orders, you know.

Sally: Doctor, do release me.

Jones: Again I say we must continue with our experiment.

Harley-Hoare: Then count up, count up, doctor.

Sally: Please don't pull the lever, please, please.

Harley-Hoare: Add, add.

Jones: 1,2,3,4.

Sally: PLEASE.

Jones: 5,6,7,8,9.

Sally: You swine.

Jones: 10. PULL THE RED.

Sally: Don't, don't, don't.

Jones: PULL THE RED I SAY.

Harley-Hoare: But look here, she's crying.

Jones: PULL THE RED, I COMMAND YOU.

Harley-Hoare: This is the last time then. But do give her the numbers again.

Sally: I'm not going to try. I refuse. I won't. I —

Jones: 799, 899, 999. (*pause*) 1,2,3,4,5,6,7,8.

Sally: 2757.

Jones: Wrong. PULL.

(Harley-Hoare *pulls the red lever and as the red light goes on and* Sally *screams.* Harley-Hoare *puts his hand over his face till scream ends. Then as light fades* Harley-Hoare *turns and quickly exits.*)

Where are you going? Wait a sec. (*pause*) Well Sally, what do you think of that? At least he's the first one that's run out on us.

Sally: Better than some I suppose, but still bloody awful. I honestly think he went on with it out of politeness — not to offend you.

Jones: He was just nervous. He had a lot of conflict.

Sally; Yes, nervous, like someone dropping a hydrogen bomb or someone with mild respectable scruples engaging in a lynching. Get me out of this.

(Sally *is released by* Jones.)

Jones: Funny, when I first heard you screaming at the rehearsal I didn't think I could manage the experiment. I suppose you get used to everything.

Sally: I don't. I can't get used to the barbarity of apparently decent human beings. Dr Jones, who can you trust?

Jones: There have been many people — even in Nazi Germany, who did obey their own consciences. Not many — but there were some. Sooner or later one person coming here will refuse to pull down the levers.

Sally: That's the only person I would trust. I think I'll have a drink.

Jones: This time of the morning?

Sally: I need it.

(*As* Sally *is taking a swig enter* Dr Daly *with* Harley-Hoare.)

Jones: Ah. (*to* Sally) You can go now. Thank you very much.

Daly: Mr Harley-Hoare just wanted to know if you were all right.

Sally: (*quietly*) You bastard.

Harley-Hoare: You were so stupid. Why didn't you add up? You didn't even try.

(*Exit* Sally.)

She didn't even try, did she, Dr Jones?

Daly: Just a few questions.

Harley-Hoare: Did you hear what she called me?

Daly: First of all we just want to thank you for your co-operation.

Harley-Hoare: Not at all, doctor. Glad to help. But I must say she was a worthless woman.

118

Daly: How do you mean?

Harley-Hoare: Very poor material.

Daly: I expect you hurt her a great deal — inflicted a great deal of pain.

Harley-Hoare: I only did what Dr Jones asked me to.

Jones: Quite right. Dr Daly, he just obeyed my commands.

Daly: But these shocks were pretty terrific and she did ask you to stop, I gather.

Harley-Hoare: I think she made a meal of it, you know. Made it sound worse than it was. Of course I realise it must have hurt a bit. I mean you know best about this learning process — I don't understand these things. I admit it got a bit rough at the end, still it was in a good cause, wasn't it?

Jones: Oh yes.

Harley-Hoare: You devised the experiment.

Daly: Yes, I did.

Harley-Hoare: I mean it was your reponsibility. I just did as I was told.

Jones: Quite — and you did it well.

Harley-Hoare: Thank you. I'm afraid I was a bit green at the beginning, a bit bungling I fear.

Jones: Next time you wouldn't make any mistakes, even little ones.

Harley-Hoare: No, no. If you want me to help out again I'm sure I'll be on song, as it were. Ye-es, she put it on a bit, definitely. That sort of woman.

Daly: It was very good of you to come along. Now if we go out to the office we'll pick up that little cheque.

Harley-Hoare: Not at all. Only too glad to be of help.

(*He puts out his hand.* Daly *hesitates, then shakes hands. They all begin to exit.*)

Harley-Hoare: I feel extraordinarily hungry. I don't know why.

Jones: Hungry?

Harley-Hoare: Famished.

(*Exit. Lights down.*)

ACT TWO

Scene One

(Liz's *flat. Darkness. Spot comes slowly up left on* Sally *asleep on the divan. As she dreams she is restless. Soon there is a sound of voices on tape whispering*.)

Kurt: (*on tape whispering*) Add 34, 35, 36, 37, 38.

The rest of the cast: (*on tape whispering*) 1,2,3,4,5,6,7,8,9,10.

Kurt: (*on tape louder*) 1,2,3,4,5,6,7,8,9,10.

All: (*on tape*) 1,2,3,4,5,6,7,8,9,10.

(*On the tape now* Sally *is heard screaming which is immediately followed by all the rest of the cast laughing loudly.* Sally *on the bed is again restless, and the lights now come up on the rest of the cast right stage standing silently in odd postures giving the whole scene a sense of unreality, e.g.* Daly *is in white coat with his mouth open, his eyes wide, staring. Suddenly* Kurt *moves like an automaton towards* Sally *on the bed*.)

Daly: (*calling*) That girl idolises you, Kurt.

Gordon: (*calling*) Kurt!

(Kurt, *hearing* Gordon's *voice, stops advancing towards* Sally. Gordon *moves towards* Kurt *in the same mechanical odd way*.)

You're wrong. She does not idolise you. -

Kurt: (*turning towards Gordon*) Well, perhaps.

Gordon: (*threateningly*) Who's wrong?

(*Now for the rest of the dream scene* Daly, Jones, Liz, Nurse *and* Harley-Hoare *act like a kind of Chorus of which* Gordon *is the dominant and bullying leader*.)

Kurt: Well . . .

Gordon: What's good for your health?

Kurt: Me.

(*All laugh until* Gordon *raises his hand*.)

Gordon: What's good for your health?

Kurt: Tomato soup.
Gordon: Celery soup.
Kurt: Ye-es, celery soup.
　　(Kurt *looks around the theatre.*)
It's just that there's a fly in here.
Liz: He's playing dodo.
Harley-Hoare: Get his head boiled.
Jones: Get him crossed off the register.
Nurse: Ask him his favourite colour.
Kurt: Yellow.
Nurse: His favourite flower.
Kurt: Carnations, Gordon.
Gordon: What's the best month in the year?
Kurt: December.
Gordon: (*yelling*) September, September, September.
Kurt: I meant September.
Gordon: What's good for your health?
Kurt: Tomato soup.
Gordon: (*shouting*) Tomato soup?
Kurt: Celery soup.
Gordon: Wrong. Onion soup. ONION SOUP.
　　(*All laugh until* Gordon *raises his hand to stop them.*)
Gordon: And the clock's ticking too loud.
Nurse: The roof's leaking.
Harley-Hoare: There's a shadow under the table.
Daly: My egg's underdone.
Jones: My toast's burnt.
Liz: It's nag, nag, nag.
Jones: My toast's black.
All: Black, black, black, black.
　　(Gordon *laughs silently, hissing. The others pick up the hissing note. All hiss.*)
Liz: Gas.
All: Gas. Gas. Gas. Gas.
Harley-Hoare: Your servant, sir. Your most obedient servant, sir.
Daly: (*pointing at* Sally) Strike her off the books.
Harley-Hoare: Expel her from the party.
　　(*The 'Chorus' now move, their hands to their necks, as if they were drowning.*)

121

All: Gas. Gas. Gas. Gas. Gas.

(Gordon *raises his hand commandingly and immediately they stop speaking and moving.*)

Kurt: But I like roses.

Gordon: (*threateningly*) Carnations are better than roses.

Kurt: Maybe.

Gordon: Your favourite colour?

Kurt: Red.

Gordon: I like yellow.

Kurt: Lot to be said for yellow.

Gordon: Yellow's the best.

Kurt: Lovely colour yellow.

Gordon: It's better than lovely.

Kurt: Yes, yellow's first.

Gordon: Better than first.

Kurt: Yellow's supreme.

Gordon: Kurt.

Kurt: Yellow's the best colour in the world.

Harley-Hoare: Please don't raise your voice.

Daly: No violence please.

Nurse: No coughing.

Kurt: But I liked her in her dark red skirt.

Harley-Hoare: (*suddenly raising his arms like an orator*) Listen. Listen, I say. (*screaming*) Listen to my message.

Liz: Speak up.

Jones: What's your message?

Harley-Hoare: Listen.

(Harley-Hoare *begins to bark like a dog and all laugh.*)

Nurse: The message of the revolutionary party. Where's Enoch? Where the devil is Enoch?

(Gordon *raises his hand and there is silence.*)

Gordon: Your favourite colour?

Kurt: Yellow.

Gordon: Red.

Kurt: Red.

Gordon: Blue, I say.

Kurt: Blue's my favourite colour.

Gordon: No, black.

Kurt: Yes, black, black, black.

Gordon: Your favourite flower?

Kurt: Carnations?

Gordon: No.

Kurt: Roses.

Gordon: No.

Kurt: Black roses?

Gordon: No. Daisies! Daisies! Daisies!

Kurt: Black daisies. I love her black daisies.

Gordon: Good boy, now you've got it. The twist of vision. Now you're talking. Now you can see in the dark. Good boy.

(Gordon *signals to 'Chorus'*.)

All: (*satirically*) Go-od boy.

Kurt: (*joyful*) Luminous black daisies. Huge funeral, rain-washed, black daisies.

(Gordon *slowly claps*. Kurt *and then 'Chorus' all join him in clapping*. Kurt *rushes to a raised level on the stage*.)

Where are they working — in the Midlands, in Yorkshire — there they are in the mill, in the factory, in the foundry, in the brick kiln.

(*General hubbub and consternation*.)

For the white worker has put on his white collar and journeyed South East.

Nurse: Sieg Heil, Sieg Heil, Sieg . . . .

Gordon: Shut up.

Nurse: (*turning round and round like a mechanical doll*) Quisling. White wog. Knock his knockers off. Knock his knockers off. Knock his knockers off. Knock his knockers off. Knock his knockers . . . .

Gordon: Shut up.

Kurt: The next time you wake up in the night and turn to the wall think of the black man.

Daly: (*chanting*) Insomnia, insomnia. Sodium amytal.

Jones: (*chanting*) Seconal, nembutal, pheno- . . . .

Gordon: Shut up.

Kurt: It's the black man who's working the nightshift when the comfortable whites are always in their comfortable beds.

(*General hubbub and consternation*.)

Tell me, who right now is cleaning the lavatories in our government offices or right here in this hospital?

Daly: Let me answer that.

Jones: Yes, Dr Daly, answer him.

Daly: I'll tell you what science says about that and about all your problems.

(*Consternation.*)

Harley-Hoare: Quiet for the doctor.

All: Give him the floor, give him the floor.

Daly: What I'm trying to tell you, if you'll listen, is plain — absolutely plain, if you follow my meaning — and if you don't, well, don't hesitate to interrupt — for what I'm saying is — is that it's like a what-do-you-call-it, honestly.

Gordon: That's too high falutin' for me.

Kurt: Too high falutin', you hear what the boss says. Tell us straight.

Daly: What I'm telling you, what I've been trying to say is scientific, if you follow me, and I'll only be too happy to explain.

(*Now speaks so fast that he becomes unintelligible and almost goes berserk. Then the actor should stop adlibbing and continue with . . . .*)

So just don't nod your head and smile now, as if you understand, and all that crap, for it's a kind of white-washing as a matter of fact.

Gordon: Get to the point, get to the point.

Kurt: You heard him. Get to the scientific point.

Harley-Hoare: Don't talk to the doctor that way.

Daly: (*quickly and wildly*) Thank you. Now to continue what I was saying without in any way trying to inconvenience you and all that, or if you happen to see what I mean in the first place, you would agree, wouldn't you, that it's so damned difficult not to be misunderstood. I mean, if I said blood is vermilion, for Pete's sake, or something like that, I could lead you astray.

Jones: We're ready, Dr Daly. We understand. Lead us astray.

Nurse: I wear two pairs of knickers.

(*Pause.*)

Daly: 34 and 35 and 36 and 37 and 38.

Kurt: I'll pull the lever.

All: 1,2,3,4,5,6,7,8,9,10.

Kurt: Let me pull the lever.

All: 1,2,3,4,5,6,7,8,9,10.

Gordon: Get her, get her.

(*All advance towards Sally on the bed.*)

Nurse: White wog, nigger lover.

124

Kurt: (*chanting*) Pull the black lever. Pull the black lever. Pull the black lever. Trust me. Pull the black lever. Pull the black lever. Pull the black lever.

(*Now on tape also and as lights dim all are heard chanting as they exit.*)

All: Trust me. Pull the black lever. Pull the black lever. Pull the black lever. Trust me. Kill the nigger lover. Kill the nigger lover. Trust us. Kill the nigger lover.

(*Voices now gradually become whisperings.*)

Kill the nigger lover. Kill the nigger lover. Trust us.

(*Doorbell rings. Lights come up on* Sally *on bed, otherwise stage empty. Enter* Liz.)

Liz: Sally.

(Sally *wakes up.*)

Sally: What? What?

Liz: I'd better answer the door. Your boy friend's here already.

Sally: My God, what time is it?

Liz: Don't worry. The dinner's almost ready.

(*Doorbell rings again.*)

Liz: It's all right. I'll get it.

(*Exit* Liz. *Pause. Lights down to darkness.*)

Scene Two

(*Spotlight right stage on* Dr Daly *not now wearing a white coat. He is standing before a lectern and occasionally refers to a paper or notes in front of him.*)

Daly: . . . And now I come to the last section of my lecture, ladies and gentlemen, which will be non-technical. As I was saying, the calamities of our recent past, the consideration of them is barely supportable. We hardly think about them but they are always with us. We're all involved, every one of us, however far removed from those scenes of bleak, pale crimes. Most of us, at this Society, are engaged, one way or another, in scientific research, but we're all, metaphorically speaking, survivors. We have lived through Auschwitz and Belsen, Hiroshima and Nagasaki, and we did not know the enormity of the offence. We were not there. But with the passing of the years these catastrophes do not recede into history, do not become a mere tale in a story book. On the contrary, as the years pass, we hear more, learn more significant details. The actual survivors tell their terrible stories of gold from teeth, of lampshades from human skin and so the abstract geography of hell becomes concrete: we see the belching smoke of the chimneys, we hear the hiss of the gas and the dying cries of the murdered. We may not be able to hold steady, in the front of our minds, the enormity of the offence for very long. The picture slips away in the silence between two heartbeats. We cannot continually retain in our minds, as we perceive the natural beauty of the earth or are touched by the genuine tenderness of lovers and friends, the psychotic savagery of our twentieth century life. No, we can't look too long at the searchlights of Auschwitz or at the coloured, intense flash of light over Hiroshima. We repress the horror. It becomes a numb disaster. In order to continue living as happily as possible, the more we need it to stay numb. It's not wrong to do that, indeed we have no choice. All the same, we do have a continual headache that we rarely discern,

(Dr Daly *hesitates, sips from a glass of water before he continues.*)

I see, near the front here, Professor Weiss who is, as we all know, amongst the most eminent of social psychologists. Well, he, amongst others, may have pointed out that the 'typical' German may be self-important, insecure, over respectful to authority, over-docile to superiors, and a little tyrant to his inferiors in the social scale. But we are not convinced that these faults are peculiar to them alone. I see you're shaking your head, Professor Weiss. Of course, I know that you don't hold that stereotyped view of Germans . . . . The Geman may have that unattractive gift for planning meticulously, they may have a need for obsessional organisation — and this, analytically speaking, does point to suppressed powerful forces within — of anarchy and division. Because of the presence of such forces, needing order, they may well have responded with a particular facility to Hitler's promise of a New Order. It's true, isn't it, that when the horns of the hunters were blowing in the dark, the German nation of 80 millions, with terrible banners unfurled, followed their raving, hysterical Führer with a sleep-walker's confidence. But despite their so-called national characteristics, their particular institutions, their history, despite Hitler and the Nazis, whose jackboots left footsteps trailing away from Auschwitz and Buchenwald, despite all this, of course they are not a special people with different chromosomes any more than the Jews, or others are, whom they murdered.

(Dr Daly *again stops to sip water.*)

Some years ago you may recall that Dr Hannah Arendt addressed this Society at our annual dinner. Since then, somewhat late, I fear, I've read Hannah Arendt's book on the *Trial of Adolf Eichmann*. It was a depressing book — if only because we learn that, with a few important exceptions, nation after nation turned on its scapegoats with a mercilessness and brutality that sometimes shocked, in its openness, even the German SS. The willingness of apparently ordinary people to obey evil commands is not a specifically German phenomenon but the record of Germany remains, and it is a shameful one. Some will forgive and most will feel no longer vengeful. Others will join with Heine to say: "Mine is a most peaceful disposition. My wishes are: a humble cottage with a thatched roof, but a good bed, good food, the freshest milk and butter, flowers before my window, and a few fine trees before my door; and if God wants to make my happiness complete, he will grant me the joy of seeing some six or seven of my enemies hanging from those trees. Before their death," continued Heine, "I shall be moved in my heart to forgive them all the wrong they did me in their lifetime. One must, it's true, forgive one's enemies — but not before they've been hanged."

(Dr Daly *smiles and nods at audience. Then looks at his watch.*)

In the few moments available to me I just want to reiterate that we have no inborn tendency, German and non-German alike, to obey orders. On the contrary, we are born saying, 'No' to civilization's imperatives. But from babyhood on we're conditioned to say, 'Yes', to obey. We are trained by punishment and reward, by threat and promise . . . . When we were small our parents proscribed our instinctual actions because they wished us not to be anti-social or because they were worried lest we damage ourselves. If we obeyed them no harm would befall us, we'd be rewarded. Our parents would smile upon us and love us. If, however, we rebelled, atrocious things may happen to us physically and we'd lose the love of those two people whom we most needed. There was no actual choice, of course. We, the little barbarians, had to become civilised or else. Else we'd be unloved, castrated, killed. "If you touch that," the six foot high voice said, "you'll be electrocuted. Come away this minute. I'll beat you, I'll not love you any more." That six foot high voice knew best: it was omnipotent. It was law and order. It was the voice of spoil-sport, bearded Moses coming down the mountain, with the Ten Commandments slipping from his hand as he shouted, "Don't," as we danced so happily, with such clear vivacity and happiness around the golden calf. From the beginning, then, disobedience is associated in our minds with fearful consequences, even death. No wonder most hardly operate their consciences as they react to a command from some apparently respectable authority. So we press down a lever or turn up a switch, obey this order or that in My Lai or in Ulster. Consciences, even where they are in operation, are remarkably soluble. That brings me back to the beginning of my talk when I discussed the remarkable experiment that took place at Yale University, the experiment devised by Professor Stanley Milgram who was interested scientifically in 'the compulsion to do evil' and how men would obey commands that were in strong conflict with their conscience. Now as an imaginative extension of his work we're carrying out a further experiment at our laboratory. At present we are using men but later will invite only women volunteers. It's too early to discuss our results, of course, but one conclusion remains evident. It is this: whether in Britain, in America, or in Germany, we should praise the ironic, indeed holy, practice of James Joyce who took as his slogan Satan's 'Non Serviam': 'I will not obey.' Thank you, Ladies and Gentlemen.

(Dr Daly *bows his head slightly and nods, smiling, as if receiving applause. Spotlight down as lights come up on Act Two, Scene Three.*)

Scene Three

(*The living room in* Liz's *house as in Act Two, Scene One.* Sally, Kurt *and* Liz *are just finishing dinner. There are empty plates, empty bottles of wine on the table, etc.*)

128

Sally: And you really think that by knowing what a man admires you can judge that man?

Kurt: It's one indication.

Sally: Then what do you admire?

Kurt: (*rising*) Oh, I dunno. Maybe the brave concealment of a personal tragedy.

Sally: (*also rising*) I don't think that tells anybody much about you.

Kurt: And I admire your cooking too, Liz. That was a great meal.

Liz: My friend, the American, he admires m-m-me. Can't say that puts him up in my estimation. Or anybody else's.

Sally: You should have asked him round, Liz.

Liz: His wife had prior claims.

Kurt: You didn't say he was married.

Liz: There's no point in committing adultery unless you're m-m-married. (*getting up*) He's so predictable. Every time he decides to make a pass at me he takes his glasses off. His eyes go soft and his right hand reaches for m-m-my left ber-ber-ber-ber . . . tit. He's so damn predictable.

Sally: That's not such a terrible thing — to be predictable I mean.

Liz: Well, you're predictable sometimes. I know that when you're skint you'll start taking taxis and begin sending telegrams like m-m-mad. And you'll eat in the best restaurants.

Sally: I don't do that when I can *afford* to get food poisoning.

Kurt: That's a typical Sally remark. You *are* afraid of being poisoned.

Sally: How do you mean?

Kurt: In some ways you were being dead serious about food poisoning.

Sally: You should tell more jokes, Kurt.

Kurt: No, the danger in that is someone may come back and tell me one. Like I said earlier, we all have to live in perpetual trust. I go into a chip shop, a transport café, or for that matter to the Savoy, and I don't expect to go down with typhoid. I go to the dentist occasionally and I trust him not to drill holes in perfectly good teeth. I have a haircut and I rely on the barber not to cut my ears off. But Sally now, she distrusts everybody and everything.

Liz: You put your car into a garage for servicing and you expect the man to check everything properly. B-brakes, tyres, everything.

Kurt: Exactly.

Liz: You're b-b-bloody crazy!

Sally: You think I don't trust *you*. That's what you're saying.

(Kurt *lights a big cigar*.)

Liz: I think the devil smokes cigars. If the devil came in right now he'd be wearing evening dress and he'd be smoking a cigar. Very suave is the devil. Wearing a carnation in his lapel and playing the xylophone.

Kurt: I just think that you're suspicious of the whole human race.

Sally:(*strongly*) I am, I am, I am. So what? Haven't I the right? Napalm, H bombs, concentration camps, private little tortures out of sight, in the dark, in the corners of the world.

Liz: You trust Fidel Castro, Sally.

Kurt: No, you're just innately suspicious, Sal. Whenever someone says something nice to you, you smell a rat.

Sally: (*smiling*) Not fair.

Kurt: I think before you'll say you'll marry me and come to the States, I'll have to undergo some holy test. Slay a dragon, kill the devil. Smash his xylophone. Save the fair maiden in her tower.

(Sally *is no longer smiling and involuntarily she stands up, seems troubled*.)

Liz: I wish someone would ask me to m-m-m-m-marry him. He could trust me.

Kurt: Of course.

Liz: He could trust m-m-me to say yes.

Kurt: I tell you one thing I admire. Something I've admired, never forgotten. It was a bowl I saw once in Copenhagen. (*very hesitantly, slowly*, Kurt *seems happy*) In a museum. A green bowl in a glass. I've never seen such a green. A wonderful green. Green you can't imagine — you just can't imagine. I walked round and round this glass case. It was a green — indescribable. Such a light green, I just stared and stared and then I heard the attendant behind say something.

(Kurt *seems abstracted now and* Liz *and* Sally *are looking at him gently smiling*.)

Whatever he said was in Danish. I said I'm from England. Then he spoke in English. Such a wonderful green, I said. It's Ming, he said. Oh, what a green, really you don't know. So luminous, so . . . that light green. Such an indescribable green. *I've never forgotten that green.*

Liz: Give me a cigar, will you?

Kurt: What?

Liz: Can you spare a cigar?

Kurt: Sure. (*offering cigar*) Are you accustomed to smoking cigars?

Liz: I used to all the time before I went to a psychiatrist . . . because of my stutter.

Kurt: He didn't help.

Liz: The psychiatrist? No, not much. But I did him a power of good. (*lights up*) This will turn me green. Indescribable green.

Sally: Know what I did today, Kurt? I took part in an experiment in a test. I wonder how you would come out in such a test?

Kurt: You slew a dragon?

Liz: This is be-b-b-better than hash. Have a go at this, Sal. Join us in our religious rite.

Kurt: What was this test then?

Sally: It doesn't matter.

Kurt: Go on.

Sally: Forget it.

Kurt: Now isn't that a bloody irritating thing? You start something and . . . .

(Sally *goes over to him and suddenly takes his hand and kisses it.*)

Liz: (*pause*) Oh my God this cigar is b-b-b-big.

Sally: That's what you did to Gordon, didn't you?

Kurt: What?

Sally: Kiss his hand.

Kurt: For crying out loud.

Liz: Come on, chaps. No quarrelling in front of the host.

Sally: Sorry, It's just . . . just that I'm tired. I . . . this experiment I took part in today. I feel tired.

Kurt: What was it anyway?

Liz: Tell us about it.

Sally: . . . well, sometime ago they set up an experiment at Yale University — in a psychological laboratory. More than a thousand people participated — and afterwards the whole thing was repeated at several other American Universities. Now a couple of London doctors have devised their own experiment and . . . .

Kurt: What's the point of it?

Sally: It's just a study of memory and learning in which one person is designated as the teacher and the other as the learner. It's all concerned with the effects of what doctors call negative reinforcement.

Liz: That's as clear as m-m-mud. Crystal clear, isn't it, Kurt?

Sally: The learner is seated in a chair and his arms strapped to stop him moving. Then an electrode is attached to his wrist. He's given a shock every time he makes an error. A mathematical error.

Kurt: Charming.

Sally: The learner is conditioned to add up correctly and quickly.

Liz: Sounds bonkers to me.

Kurt: And today you went along as one of those er, teachers?

Sally: Right.

Kurt: How did you get involved in it?

Sally: Oh, some chap I know asked me if I'd volunteer. They need volunteers badly.

Kurt: You're just an inveterate do-gooder.

Sally: They're just short of people, that's all. It was very interesting as a matter of fact. I said I'd try and find other people to volunteer as teachers.

Liz: OK. Count me in. Sounds b-b-better than giving b-b-blood. Especially *my* ber-ber-ber . . . .

Sally: No, they want men. They need men very badly, Kurt.

Liz: M-me too.

Sally: Pack it in, Liz.

Kurt: You want me to volunteer?

Sally: Well, they're very short of people tomorrow.

Kurt: Is it in the daytime?

Sally: Yeh.

Kurt: It's difficult. I've got to be in the office. Besides — well quite honestly — some of these psychological learning tests don't sound very sensible.

Sally: But I promised, Kurt.

Kurt: You promised what?

Sally: All of us promised. Each one of us said that we would get one other person to come along to the laboratory. Please, Kurt.

Kurt: You said something about a test. You said you wondered how I would fare in some sort of test. Is this it?

Sally: No. I didn't explain it properly. They'll explain it to you. Just let me ring them up and say you'll come tomorrow afternoon.

Kurt: Will you be there?

Sally: No, no. I have to be at the theatre. We have a run through tomorrow. It's an important rehearsal tomorrow.

(*Pause.*)

Kurt: OK. If you want me to. If you really want me to go along, I will. I suppose I can take the afternoon off.

Sally: Thank you, Kurt.

Liz: Well, how about some coffee?

Sally: I'll make it.

Liz: No, I'll do it.

Sally: You made the dinner. Kurt and I will fix it. You take it easy, put your feet up.

(Sally *takes* Kurt's *hand and they begin to exit to kitchen.*)

Liz: You don't need two people to put the kettle on.

Sally: We do, love. Me to turn the gas on and Kurt to strike a match.

(Kurt *and* Sally *embrace.*)

Liz: I have the distinct feeling you two want me to be alone.

Sally: By the way, Kurt, when you go along to the laboratory, I'd rather you didn't mention my name.

Kurt: Why ever not?

(*Exit* Kurt *and* Sally. Liz *picks up a journal, looks fed up. Lights gradually come down to darkness.*)

Scene Four

(*When lights rise again we are in* Mr Harley-Hoare's *office.* Harley-Hoare *is banging successive papers with rubber stamp when* Kurt *enters.*)

Kurt: Busy?

Harley-Hoare: Just giving these the old rubber stamp.

Kurt: I'm off to Dr Daly's laboratory this afternoon.

(Harley-Hoare *suddenly stops.*)

I understand you've been. My secretary told me.

Harley-Hoare: It was confidential.

Kurt: Oh, I'm sorry. She didn't even tell me confidentially.

(Harley-Hoare *resumes rubber stamping.*)

It doesn't matter me knowing, does it? I mean I'm volunteering myself and I'm not keeping it a secret. I have to go shortly, and I'm curious to know how you made out.

Harley-Hoare: A.1. Very well. Definitely. Yes, it was a challenge.

Kurt: Can't you get one of the younger clerks to do that?

Harley-Hoare: You can't trust the youngsters these days. You have to do everything yourself.

Kurt: Still they couldn't go far wrong with that could they?

Harley-Hoare: (*momentarily stops banging*) They could get it upside down, sir. (*continues stamping*) They're just clock watchers nowadays. They just come into the office to let their hair grow. Very poor material.

Kurt: I gather that one has to pull down different levers which give the student a shock when he makes a mistake.

Harley-Hoare: Student?

Kurt: They are students, aren't they?

Harley-Hoare: The one I had didn't exactly look like a student. A strident bag, she was. Still these days . . . students! Some of them, the way they behave, deserve a few shocks. Too clever by half, some of them, with Trotsky this and Ché that.

Kurt: Well, students ought to be bright.

Harley-Hoare: Quite right, sir.

Kurt: And one expects them to be rebellious and to be concerned with moral issues.

Harley-Hoare: Oh yes, I have a great respect for students.

(*Enter* Gordon. *Immediately* Harley-Hoare *bangs the papers at an increased rate.*)

Gordon: Ah Kurt, there you are. I want you to come to the conference at 4.

Kurt: Can't. Sorry, Gordon.

Gordon: What?

Kurt: I've promised to be elsewhere.

134

Gordon: (*to* Harley-Hoare) What are you doing?

Harley-Hoare: Pardon?

Gordon: What the hell are you up to?

Harley-Hoare: I'll be through with this in a tick, sir.

    (Harley-Hoare *is now banging papers at an incredible rate.*)

Gordon: Stop it. STOP IT.

Harley-Hoare: Beg your pardon, but I . . . .

Gordon: Now Kurt, what's this about not coming to the conference?

Kurt: I've promised to go to the hospital.

Harley-Hoare: To see Dr Daly. He's volunteered for the experiment.

Gordon: *You?*

Kurt: Yes, why not? Do you know about Dr Daly's set up?

Gordon: Who suggested *you* should volunteer?

Kurt: Sally Parsons. Why?

    (Gordon *suddenly laughs silently.*)

Gordon: That's a good one. Ha, ha, ha.

Kurt: What's funny?

Gordon: Sally Parsons suggested you should volunteer to give her electric shocks. Ha, ha, ha. that's rich, that's gravy rich. Kinky. Ha, ha, ha.

Kurt: What's the big joke? She volunteered to pull down the levers. Now I am.

Gordon: Ha, ha, ha. It's very funny.

Harley-Hoare: Ha, ha, ha. It is funny. It's very funny, isn't it sir? Ha, ha, ha.

Gordon: (*stops laughing*) What is?

Harley-Hoare: That we should all . . . well . . . happen to volunteer.

Gordon: Your girl friend never volunteered, Kurt. She'll be sitting in the chair. She wants you to shock her to hell, don't you see? She's testing you out. Testing to see whether you'll be brute enough to give her maximum shocks like this, this runt did probably.

Harley-Hoare: Brute enough? *Brute enough?*

Kurt: I don't understand.

Harley-Hoare: Who is this Sally Parsons? Was she the woman in the chair?

Gordon: That's right. The lady in the chair — I'll spell it out for you — was sweet little, kinky little Sally bloody Parsons, ha, ha, ha. She's a good friend of Mr Jennings here. A very good friend, and by profession an actress. And you thought you gave her shocks. Only you didn't.

Harley-Hoare: I gave her shocks all right, oh brother I gave her shocks. She was screaming. I'm telling you she raised the roof. She was no friend of Mr Jennings. I'm sure of that. She wasn't . . . no, no, the type.

Gordon: It wasn't really wired up, you pretentious git. You pulled down the levers and she screamed very convincingly, that's all. She's an actress, Mr Harley-Hoare, an actress. And no doubt she can scream like any good woman.

Harley-Hoare: An actress?

Kurt: It's absurd Gordon. What the hell are you suggesting? Sally knows I wouldn't give her shocks.

Harley-Hoare: It's to do with the learning process, Dr Daly told me.

Kurt: Yes, with conditioning — Sally said so. It's a psychological learning test.

Gordon: (*to Harley-Hoare*) Yes, they are learning how men like you will obey commands however evil, they are confirming that ordinary citizens like you will destroy people if they see it as a duty and if they are ordered to do so by some higher authority.

Harley-Hoare: (*loudly*) What is this?

Kurt: (*louder*) What's the learning process to do with acting? Or with Sally?

Gordon: Don't you understand yet?

Harley-Hoare: That middle-aged woman in the chair was no actress. I can tell an actress from a . . . listen I'm no baby in nappies when it comes to actresses.

Kurt: You're lying Gordon. What game are you playing?

Gordon: Ha, ha, ha.

Harley-Hoare: When I was in the RAF I was on the entertainments committee at my last station. They sent these troupers round. Real troupers. At the camp cinema there was a bit of a stage and in the spotlight they'd bash out their acts, singing the old songs for the boys, Paper Doll, Starlight.

Kurt: Just a minute.

Harley-Hoare: Smoke gets in your Eyes, Sophisticated Lady.

Kurt: (*loud*) Just a second.

136

Harley-Hoare: Can't get Indiana off my Mind. Very accomplished.

Kurt: You said it was a middle-aged lady in the chair?

Harley-Hoare: As a matter of fact I dealt with these people personally. I can tell an actress from a . . .

Gordon: Human being? Ha, ha, ha.

Kurt: Middle-aged, Gordon. The lady in the chair was middle-aged.

Gordon: Ha, ha, ha.

Kurt: Are you trying to suggest I wouldn't recognise her, that Sally is so made up that — (*shakes his head, baffled*)

Harley-Hoare: With a wig? Are you telling me it's a wig?

Gordon: That's what I'm telling you both.

Harley-Hoare: (*loud*) But you fixed it for me. You spoke to Dr Daly on my behalf. You cheated . . . . You rotten swi . . . .

Gordon: Yes?

Harley-Hoare: That woman. This Sally Parsons. She doesn't *deserve a Christian burial.*

Kurt: Go to hell, Gordon. GO TO HELL.

Gordon: Actresses, you see. One minute they're Virgin Queens in great marble palaces and the next they're penniless poxed whores in a doss house. Well, that's great. But in between times, Kurt, they're nothing. They have no identity at all. You want to marry a woman like that Kurt? You want to marry someone who wants to make quite sure you are not an incipient Nazi before she signs on the dotted line?

(*Suddenly* Harley-Hoare *picks up rubber stamp and bangs at the papers.* Kurt *and* Gordon *stare at him, then* Kurt *turns on his heel and exits.*)

(*Calling*) Kurt. It's for the best, Kurt. (*pause*) Yes, it's a stroke of luck. Do stop banging away. (*pause*) Please. Oh, come on, Mr Harley-Hoare, stop sulking.

(Harley-Hoare *stops.*)

Harley-Hoare: I'm bitterly disappointed.

Gordon: What about?

Harley-Hoare: It's not fair, sir.

Gordon: But I'm pleased with you.

Harley-Hoare: Pleased?

Gordon: Sure I am. Give me a cigarette, will you? I left mine on my desk.

Harley-Hoare: You misled me. You do owe me an apology.

Gordon: Oh, I see. You want to resign?

Harley-Hoare: Resign? Well . . . I hadn't thought.

Gordon: Do think, do think.

> (Harley-Hoare *brings out his cigarettes and tentatively offers* Gordon *one*. Gordon *smiles, takes one*.)

So you want your cards? Have you a light?

Harley-Hoare: I've worked here a long time, Mr Gordon. But really, I don't know what to say. *An actress.*

Gordon: I'd appreciate it if you didn't tell anybody that Dr Daly is using an actress. You see, it's a medical secret.

Harley-Hoare: Oh quite. You can depend on me sir. All the same you took me in and I feel . . . misused.

Gordon: I couldn't tell you, don't you see? I mean medical confidences have to be kept.

Harley-Hoare: I respect that but . . .

Gordon: So I hardly owe you an apology.

Harley-Hoare: On the other hand.

Gordon: You still think that I have malignantly misled you?

Harley-Hoare: I wouldn't say that.

Gordon: You think the worst of me?

Harley-Hoare: No, no, sir, no.

Gordon: You thought the worst of me?

Harley-Hoare: Of course not.

Gordon: You did.

Harley-Hoare: If you think I thought that, well, I'm very sorry. I'm very sorry I gave you that impression, sir.

Gordon: Are you apologising to me then?

Harley-Hoare: Certainly. It was very wrong of me to jump to conclusions. I do apologise. Medical confidential, quite.

Gordon: But you still want your cards?

> (Harley-Hoare *suddenly leaps forward with a light for* Gordon's *cigarette*.)

Thank you.

Harley-Hoare: No, no, under the circumstances I'd be grateful if . . . . I don't want my cards, no, no. Why should I? You accept my apology, sir?

Gordon: So you don't want your cards?

Harley-Hoare: No.

Gordon: But you want a rise?

Harley-Hoare: A rise? No, no. A rise, heavens no.

Gordon: Ha, ha, ha. I'm pleased with you. Ha, ha, ha. I'm pleased with everything. Why shouldn't you have your rise?

Harley-Hoare: I'm pleased if you're pleased.

Gordon: Things have worked out very well. Everything is going to be very good.

Harley-Hoare: Excellent.

Gordon: This will put the tin hat on it.

Harley-Hoare: Absolutely. (*pause*) On what, sir?

Gordon: It's great.

Harley-Hoare: Quite, I was going to say that . . . it's a great . . . day.

Gordon: You're happy here?

Harley-Hoare: Yes sir. You're happy sir? (*pause*) You said something about a rise.

Gordon: Don't you think I should give you a rise?

Harley-Hoare: If you think you should, I think you should.

Gordon: But don't you feel guilty?

Harley-Hoare: I have apologised, sir.

Gordon: I don't mean contrition. I mean guilt.

Harley-Hoare: I don't quite follow you.

Gordon: You want justice.

Harley-Hoare: *You* . . . . I can rely on you, I'm sure.

Gordon: Then you do feel guilty.

Harley-Hoare: Only generally.

Gordon: Sure, sure, generally. Like when you have refused a beggar alms.

Harley-Hoare: (*puzzled*) I suppose so.

Gordon: Yes, I understand. It's true for all of us. Afterwards we worry ourselves for a minute or two. Feel guilt. Then perhaps we reassure ourselves. Tell ourselves, *well* he was a professional beggar anyway. He would have drunk up the value of the silver coin we turned over in our pockets.

Harley-Hoare: That's it. I know that feeling.

Gordon: You do understand. You're sweating Mr Harley-Hoare.

Harley-Hoare: It's warm in here.

Gordon: It's like when you turn off the television set when they are about to show you once again the atrocities in Africa or Asia, turn off the images of starving children, the children with Belsen eyes. You don't want to see that any more so you turn the set off, right? And you feel guilty for turning the set off. Why are you sweating?

Harley-Hoare: It *is* warm in here. Very warm. I try and do my duty sir.

Gordon: You shall have justice. I'm going to raise your salary by 4 per cent. Don't you think I should?

Harley-Hoare: You know best sir.

Gordon: *It's not enough.* How about 8 per cent?

Harley-Hoare: That's very generous.

Gordon: You're pleased then? Ha, ha. Ha, ha, ha.

Harley-Hoare: You won't regret it.

Gordon: No siree, I won't. You know Harley-Hoare . . . I've done two good deeds today. I've stopped a boy making a disastrous marriage. That's worth doing, is it not? That gives me satisfaction. One day Kurt will thank me and see that my motives were pure — which they are. Yet I wonder if he'll ever believe me. She's psychologically a bad bet. Oh yes, I know all about her. I can feel pity for her. But I don't want her to marry anyone I'm fond of. I don't want Kurt crucified.

Harley-Hoare: And the second good thing is that you have raised my salary.

Gordon: That's right. At least I've made you a slightly happier man.

Harley-Hoare: That's true, and I'm grateful.

Gordon: You're an odd man, Harley-Hoare.

Harley-Hoare: Me, odd? I don't think *I'm* odd.

Gordon: Well, perhaps not. It's simply that you renew my belief in the unfathomable strangeness of every human being.

(Gordon *waves and exits and* Harley-Hoare *returns to stamping papers. After a while he stops and looks at the audience with a delighted aspect of glee on his face as lights dim for the next scene in the laboratory.*)

Scene Five

(*The Laboratory. Lights come up on* Sally *and* Dr Jones.)

Jones: I just can't allow this, you just can't manipulate our experiments in this personal way. I just have to tell Dr Daly.

Sally: It's too late now. Dr Daly would be furious. Kurt would be furious.

Jones: They both would have a right to be.

Sally: In ten minutes he'll be here. In half an hour he'll go again. No one need ever know. Kurt won't recognise me and Dr Daly will have one more statistic to add to his list. No harm will be done. *Please.* (*takes whisky flask out of her bag*) Holy Lenin, I'm sorry I told you.

Jones: You'll end up in a chronic alcoholic ward.

Sally: Please don't moralize again.

Jones: The way you've got him here with all of your . . . pretences — to test him, for heaven's sake. It would be best if you went out there now, even at this late hour.

Sally: You're so . . . chapel.

Jones: C'mon, Sally. I can only give you advice, that's all a doctor can do.

Sally: You're as hard as nails.

Jones: Me? (*laughs*) Nobody's ever accused me of that before.

Sally: I've watched you. During all those trials with the volunteers. You've been fascinated by it all, unhealthily. You stand there, always so calm, quiet, still — as if you're at a public execution. You're involved in the whole bloody thing but not as a scientist.

(Jones *turns and makes as if to exit.* Sally *calls after her.*)

Don't tell them. I told you in confidence. Yes, you're a doctor, not a priest and you can't give me absolution but I confessed to you and you have no right to go sneaking off and telling . . . .

Jones: (*loud*) Sally! (*quietly*) I won't tell anybody — but I can't have any part in this . . . deception. I'm opting out of it. Dr Daly can call out the numbers himself.

Sally: (*going to electric chair*) At least, will you strap me in?

(Jones *hesitates.*)

I'm just asking you to strap me in, that's no big deal, is it? Please, Dr Jones.

(Jones *goes over to strap* Sally *in the chair.*)

Jones: I don't think I should even be doing this.

Sally: You don't like me, do you?

Jones: Don't be daft.

Sally: I hate myself sometimes. And I know I'm stupid to act out a fairy story where the Prince has to be tested to see if he's fit for the fair maid.

Jones: Apart from what's right and what's wrong I know in my bones you're making a mistake. What if your young man does pull down all the levers? After all, statistically speaking, like so many others, your Prince could turn out to be a Frog.

Sally: You're not married, are you?

Jones: No.

Sally: Never will be, will you? (*pause*) You're stuck on Michael Daly.

Jones: Duw, you're just a child. A romantic child. And you have a genius for being wrong. (*coldly*) Tell Dr Daly I was called away and won't be back till tomorrow.

Sally: I'm not a hundred per cent sure that I want Kurt to come through as a Prince. I don't know, I don't know.

Jones: Shall I unstrap you then?

Sally: No . . . . I have to know.

Jones: Sally, the underside of fairy stories is often soaked in blood.

Sally: I'll tell Dr Daly you were called away. (*pause*) Thanks, Olwen.

Jones: Good luck.

(*Exit* Jones. Sally *in chair, closes her eyes. Soon there are voices off.*)

Daly: (*off*) No, no, nurse, you needn't bother. If you'll take these forms back to the office. Thank you. This way, Mr Jennings.

Kurt: (*off*) And it goes up you say in increments of 40 volts?

Daly: Correct. Ah, in here, Mr Jennings — after you.

(*Enter* Kurt *and* Dr Daly.)

This is our other volunteer. All ready, I see. Good.

(Kurt *keeps his distance from* Sally. *They just nod at each other.*)

And here are the levers. Would you care to inspect them, Mr Jennings?

(*While* Kurt *looks at levers* Daly *talks quietly to* Sally.)

Daly: Where's Dr Jones?

Sally: She was called away. She won't be in until tomorrow.

Daly: Oh. Everything clear, Mr Jennings?

Kurt: Very clear. And now you intend to make her add up various sums, is that right?

Daly: Uh-huh.

Kurt: And I'm to throw these levers and give her electric shocks if she makes errors.

Daly: Quite right.

Kurt: At a certain point it will cause a great deal of pain. I mean if she makes many mistakes.

Daly: Yes, she knows that.

Kurt: And she doesn't mind?

Daly: No. For this she has freely volunteered.

Kurt: (*to* Sally) You don't mind receiving even high electric shocks if you make mistakes?

(Sally *shakes her head.*)

(*To* Daly) I know scientists have trained rats to perform all kinds of rat miracles by giving them shocks.

Daly: Quite. Shall we start?

(Daly *turns all lights down so that* Sally *is now in a white spotlight.*)

Kurt: But rats aren't human beings.

Daly: Of course not. The same with drugs. Drugs are tried out on laboratory animals and all kinds of tests are conducted. There comes a time though when the laboratory animal tests have to be carried out on human beings. Medical progress can only work this way.

Kurt: No. Rats aren't human beings. Rats can't volunteer to take part in such experiments.

Daly: (*jovially*) No, that's true. Well now — all set?

Kurt: I must tell you, Dr Daly, I don't like this experiment.

Daly: Oh, but you did volunteer. Of course, if you would rather not go on with it at this late stage, then you are free to withdraw. However, I hope you will not let us down. After all, we haven't started yet. (*to* Sally) You are ready, aren't you?

(Sally *nods affirmatively.*)

Kurt: You really want to go on with this?

(Sally *just smiles.*)

Daly: Yes, she does. Now Mr Jennings, if you have any more questions I would rather you addressed them to me.

Kurt: You have explained that the reason for this experiment is to discover the relationship between punishment and the learning process — well that reason does seem laudable.

Daly: Quite. Are you ready then to start?

Kurt: But it's such a thing, such a thing, such a thing!
Daly: What?

(Kurt *turns away, his back to* Dr Daly *and* Sally.)
Daly: I really must insist either you refuse definitely to participate in this experiment or we start at once. We only have a limited time at our disposal, you see.

(*No reply from* Kurt.)
Do I understand that you won't participate in our experiment?
Kurt: (*turning*) Why not?
Daly: Very well.
Kurt: Why should I back out now? I haven't changed my mind. Nor has she changed her mind.
Daly: Then please go to the white lever.
Kurt: The first one?
Daly: Yes.
Kurt: And this white lever, that's the first one I pull down?
Daly: Yes.
Kurt: This red lever is the last one?
Daly: Yes, the red lever is the last. But as I told you — if you pull down the red lever consecutively it will increase the voltage even more than just pulling it once.
Kurt: That could be dangerous.
Daly: It has its dangers. Our subject here understands that.
Kurt: So I just pull it down (*screaming*) LIKE THIS.

(Kurt *pulls down the red lever consecutively and the red light goes on and off and on and off and on and off. We see* Sally's *face change from surprise to silent tears. She does not make a sound.* Daly *puts both arms in the air and for a moment is dumbstruck.*)
Daly: (*shouting*) Stop it. STOP IT.

(Daly *makes to put all lights on.* Kurt *comes away from the levers.*)
You're crazy, you're really crazy.
Kurt: You idiot. Don't you think I knew that this is one goddam, bloody hoax? Who the hell do you think you are?
Sally: Kurt!
Kurt: For God's sake you — *you* shut up. I tell you something, Sally, you're fouled up. You're a case and you need help.
Daly: I don't understand. I mean — you called her Sally. You know her?
Kurt: Yes, I know her. I know her too damn well.

144

Daly: Now look here . . . .

Kurt: No. You look here. Fraud is not research. You wanted me to be one of your victims, you wanted to luxuriate in the pleasure of your own personal power. With the excuse that it's for the fatherland. The fatherland of Science.

Daly: Now, come, you misunderstand. What we are doing is part of a scientific enquiry. Sally knows that even if you don't.

Sally: (*quietly*) I hate you. I hate you all. I feel so depressed. I don't know what's wrong with me. Everybody's voices are just *too loud*.

(Sally *closes her eyes.*)

Kurt: I question the moral basis of your so-called experiment. Why, you're using people like me as guinea pigs and they don't even know. You *fool* them, you manipulate them, you discomfort them.

Daly: You're confused. Are you all right Sally?

Kurt: I'm not confused. This experiment is like a practical joke. Indeed, like a practical joker you play tricks on your victims. You reduce them to fools and in so doing you assert your own power.

Daly: I'm not going to argue with you. You don't understand the mind of a scientist. He is motivated by curiosity. True, curiosity leads to knowledge and knowledge to power. But we are all threatened by our own ignorance — and it is more than power we are after. It's a sense of security that we need. For not much is visible, and not often, do you understand? The world is at war with itself because man is at war with himself. And he needs help. We all need help. Why do you think that I am a doctor?

Kurt: I understand that you don't understand your own motives. But then nor do I. (*aggressive*) Heaven knows what sort of extraordinary unconscious gratification you are getting out of these practical jokes. It's a big laugh, really, you finally fool yourself . . . .

Daly: I can't talk to you.

(*Turns on his heel and begins to exit.*)

Kurt: You don't want to hear the truth. Every person who pulls down the levers is *your victim*.

(*Exit* Daly.)

Sally: Let me go, Kurt.

Kurt: You! (*pause*) You should have trusted me.

Sally: Undo these straps, please.

145

Kurt: You put me on trial.

Sally: I know. I'm sorry.

Kurt: You're a bitch, you know that? You're a bitch in London and you'd be a bitch in New York.

Sally: I said I'm sorry. I know it was wrong, I'm sorry. I said I'm sorry, I can't say any more than sorry.

Kurt: And if I hadn't recognised you, or if I hadn't known it was you in that chair, would you still have been sorry? (*pause*) You're abrasive and difficult and sometimes you cry out like . . . I dunno . . . like an animal that's not *well*. But *this* I can't take.

Sally: Undo the straps please. Let me get out of this chair. Don't just accuse me in this chair. Look, it's not so terrible. I haven't committed a great crime.

(Kurt *goes towards her tentatively as if to release her.*)

Kurt: You don't really care for me at all.

Sally: I do, I do, John.

(Kurt *turns away as if he'd received a blow.*)

Kurt: John?

Sally: Oh my God.

Kurt: You can't do more than apologise. That's it, you can't. That's reasonable.

Sally: We could begin again, Kurt.

Kurt: So now you are calling me Kurt.

(Kurt *begins to exit.*)

Sally: Kurt!

Kurt: You *can't.*

(*Exit* Kurt.)

Sally: For pity's sake, Kurt. I'm sorry.

(*Pause as she struggles to get out of the chair and calls*)
I do need help, Kurt.

(*She struggles again with the straps.*)
Kurt! Dr Daly! Dr Daly! Help, help! Oh hell. Dr Daly! Kurt! Help! Help! HELP!

(*Lights go down and* Sally *looks upwards at fading spot and speaks quietly.*)
Oh God, help. (*pause*) I wanna die. Oh God. Pull the black lever, I wanna die.

PYTHAGORAS (SMITH)

Characters

Pythagoras (Smith)
Charlie
Dr Robert Aquillus
Nurse Grey
Marian Cunningham
Ellen
Biddy Morgan
Mr X
Ken Kennedy
Arthur Haines
Dr Bruce Green

ACT ONE

Scene One

(*The superintendent's office. On stage right is a desk with in-trays, blotting paper, telephone; on stage left is a white coat on a coat hanger. Apart from usual office furniture there is a covered parrot's cage. As the lights come up,* Pythagoras Smith, *a tall, white-faced man just under forty, is bringing up a conductor's baton over his head. As he does so, a twangy musical note becomes louder. When he slowly brings down the baton the lights lower and the twangy note softens. In short, it would appear that* Pythagoras *with his baton is controlling the degree of lighting on the stage and the loudness of the curious music. Now, as the music and lights become more powerful,* Pythagoras *looks stern.*)

Pythagoras: (*shouting*) Cease! Stop! Stop, I say!
    (*Lights become fixed. Music ceases.* Pythagoras, *delighted*

149

with his own power, smiles briefly at the audience. This time, as he brings down the baton, lights go down slowly, but the musical note begins and becomes louder and is loudest when the stage is dark.)

Pythagoras: *(above music)* Now again. C'mon, c'mon. That's it.

(As lights come on slowly and brighten, the music becomes softer and finally ceases.)

Pythagoras: Ha, ha, ha, very good, ha, ha, ha. I'm on form.

(Enter Charlie, *a short, middle-aged man who is evidently surprised to see* Pythagoras.*)*

Charlie: What's the joke, Pythagoras?

Pythagoras: Ha, ha, ha. Mornin', Charlie.

Charlie: What are you doin' in Dr Aquillus's office?

Pythagoras: What are *you* doing in Dr Aquillus's office?

Charlie: That a conductor's baton?

Pythagoras: Listen, Charlie, when I bring this cane down slowly the light will fade and you'll hear a very strange, unusual note.

Charlie: Go on.

(Pythagoras brings down baton slowly. Nothing happens. No change of light nor any sound, but Pythagoras *seems pleased.)*

Charlie: Nothing's happening.

Pythagoras: Bravo, now cease! Stop, I say. Ha, ha, ha. What do you think of that? The music of the spheres. I'll tell you the secret of how to make magic, Charlie.

Charlie: Mmm?

(pause)

Pythagoras: Think blue, say green. And squeeze apple-pips from a tangerine. Ha, ha, ha.

Charlie: Music of the spheres, my foot. Like I said to Dr Aquillus, you're just a second-class stage magician with a paid-up Equity card now in the bin with the rest of us.

Pythagoras: *(lifting baton)* Now I'll restore the sunlight. It'll be a beautiful June morning again. *(baton now over his head)* What do you think of that, eh?

Charlie: No wonder you never made the Palladium.

Pythagoras: The speed of light deceives the eye.

Charlie: You could have fooled me!

Pythagoras: If you'd studied Anaximander, read the accounts of Babylonian astronomy and Egyptian mensuration you too would have heard the music of the spheres. And I could teach even *you* how to intensify light and delete it.

Charlie: Just because you think you've been reincarnated . . . .

Pythagoras: My disciples used to say there were three kinds of rational creatures: gods, men, and those such as me, Pythagoras, first philosopher, astronomer, mathematician and magician.

Charlie: (*mockingly*) I know all about you, mate. Put on the right shoe first, wash the left foot first. No meat, no fish, no beans.

(Charlie *takes baton from* Pythagoras.)

Pythagoras: (*with dignity*) That's only partly true. I don't know where you got hold of that. But even the ancient sources that scholars use are unreliable. They listen to a little gossip in a great silence. My life story, Charlie, is a scratch on a worn stone of the sixth century BC. Yes, I — be careful with my magic cane. Don't bend it! Like the sceptre of Zeus, it's made of cypress wood.

Charlie: (*sneering*) Magic cane? Ha, ha, ha, it's from Woolworth's. Music of the stars. Ker-rist.

Pythagoras: You be careful. Careful. Magic is a primitive form of applied science and like science it gives you power.

Charlie: You call this bit of wood, this baton, magic! You're over the top, old fella. It's time you heard the truth, time . . . .

Pythagoras: (*annoyed*) My magic cane will stick to your hand. It's stuck to your hand.

Charlie: What?

Pythagoras: Throw it on the floor, you can't, you can't.

Charlie: Course I can, don't be daft.

Pythagoras: You can't get rid of it. Try it, go on, ha, ha, ha.

(Charlie *tries to throw the cane on to the floor, but it won't leave his hand.* Pythagoras *is laughing.*)

Charlie: (*mumbling*) Damn stick. It's got glue on it.

Pythagoras: Ha, ha, ha.

Charlie: (*over*) Dr Aquillus said you mustn't hypnotize any of us. He expressly said hypnotism verboten.

Pythagoras: Are you hypnotized?

Charlie: Course not.

Pythagoras: What's the temperature of that *magic* cane?

Charlie: Temperature?

Pythagoras: Don't you feel its star-like magnetic heat?

Charlie: It *is* lukewarm.

Pythagoras: It's warming up. It's getting hotter and you can't let go.

Charlie: It is getting hotter. Ouch, ouch.

Pythagoras: It's hotter still.

Charlie: Ouch, ouch! (*yells*) Aw. Crikey.

(Charlie *jumps up and down shouting.*)

Pythagoras: OK. OK. Don't make such a shindy.

Charlie: Aw, aw. I'm burning. *Burning*.

Pythagoras: It's getting cooler. It's cooling.

Charlie: Aw. Ouch. Ah.

Pythagoras: Definitely cooling. When it gets cold you'll be able to drop it on the floor.

Charlie: Yes, ah, aw, yes. Aaah.

(Charlie *drops cane. He looks at his hand*)

I'll roast you one day, Pythagoras. Look at my hand. Scalded.

(*Sound of a distant clock striking nine.*)

Pythagoras: Dr Aquillus will be here soon. We better beat it.

Charlie: I don't like Aquillus. He's stingy. Gives away nothing.

Pythagoras: Right. He only smiles in millimetres. He resembles Polycrates.

Charlie: Poly . . . who?

Pythagoras: Polycrates, tyrant of Samos, where I was born two and a half thousand years ago. Do you know what Polycrates valued most?

Charlie: Your gifts?

Pythagoras: His signet ring. I used to say, 'Friendship is Equality, Polycrates'. But he wouldn't listen. He was only interested in building the temple of Hera and constructing the great seawalls of the harbour. And a tunnel nearly a mile long to bring . . . .

(Pythagoras *suddenly and quickly exits left. He has heard the approach of the superintendent,* Dr Aquillus, *who enters right.* Dr Robert Aquillus *is a kindly, absent-minded, stooping man nearing retiring age.* Charlie *picks up baton.*)

Charlie: Pythagoras, you've left your . . . .

Aquillus: What are you doing here?

Charlie: Mornin', doctor. Come here to show you my right hand, Dr Aquillus.

Aquillus: Can't play now, Charlie. I haven't had breakfast yet.

Charlie: It's scalded.

Aquillus: What is?

(*Enter* Nurse Grey *with breakfast tray.*)

Nurse: Good morning, Dr Aquillus. Beautiful morning, Charlie.

Charlie: This conductor's baton here. It got very hot.

Nurse: Dr Aquillus has a busy day today, Charlie. The concert tonight. The madrigals to rehearse and so on. Do get *your* breakfast before the others eat it.

Aquillus: What time are the students coming from Westminster Hospital?

Nurse: Ten-thirty.

Charlie: (*loud*) Look at my hand. I bloody well order you to look at my hand. My right hand.

(Charlie *with left hand throws baton high into the air. It falls on to the floor.*)

Aquillus: Charlie seems more than usually disturbed this morning.

Nurse: Perhaps he could be your demonstration patient.

Charlie: No, don't choose me, doctor. *Please.* Choose Pythagoras. He thinks he can hypnotize people. The students would love that. My hand's OK now, don't worry. Please don't choose me.

Aquillus: I'm not going to choose you, Charlie. Relax.

Charlie: Thank you, doctor. Good doctor. Shall I take the cover off the parrot's cage for you, doctor?

Nurse: I'll do that. You go and get your breakfast.

Charlie: Thank you, doctor.

(*Exit* Charlie, *bowing.*)

(*at door*) I do like your signet ring, doctor.

(Charlie *exits.* Nurse *takes cover off parrot's cage.* Dr Aquillus *butters toast.*)

Aquillus: Illness takes the mask off people. Poor Charlie.

Nurse: There you are, Polly. There you are, isn't that better? I do wish it would answer.

Aquillus: Not one word have I got out of that parrot since it came here to The Cedars. Mute. Catatonic. It's difficult to organize a meaningful therapeutic relationship with that bird, ha ha ha.

Nurse: By the way, doctor, Marian Cunningham is anxious to know what day you're discharging her.

Aquillus: (*rising*) Is she assisting Pythagoras at the concert tonight?

Nurse: Yes.

Aquillus: That might stir her up. Better leave it till this weekend is over.

Nurse: Monday then?

Aquillus: Any day next week.

(Dr Aquillus *stares at parrot as he stands drinking his morning tea.* The Nurse, *about to leave, picks up the cane but immediately drops it as if it were red-hot.*)

Nurse: Ouch!

(*Startled by Nurse's loud cry,* Dr Aquillus *simultaneously drops his saucer.*)

Aquillus: What's the matter?

Nurse: (*looking at cane puzzled*) Oh, nothing. Just some static electricity.

(*Lights down to darkness and music up of 'These Foolish Things'.*)

Scene Two

(*The common room. The radio is playing 'These Foolish Things'. To the right is a large urn from which patients can take coffee or tea. Three women enter right to take their coffee. They are:* Biddy, *a fat, depressed woman in her thirties;* Marian, *an attractive twenty-four-year-old; and* Ellen, *an American middle-aged lady, who turns off the radio.*)

Biddy: I'm still hungry. That was a very low-caloried breakfast.

Ellen: You ate Arthur's egg besides your own. I saw you. (*pause*) To think you'll be leaving us soon, Marian. I remember your first day.

Marian: It was such a relief to be put to bed, to be looked after.

Ellen: Damn thing is they force you to get up after twenty-four hours. Go into the common room, Ellen, they said. Meet up with the others. Like a hole in the head I wanted that. I didn't wanna meet up with anybody, no Joe Blow or anybody, no sir. I need sedatives, Dr Aquillus, I said. Gimme deep sleep treatment, Bob, I said. I wanted out. Religion saved me.

Marian: (*happily*) Just think. It's over. No more group therapy. No more OT.

Ellen: I hate making baskets.

Biddy: No more set meals.

Marian: No more *regimentation*. If they'll let me I shall quit The Cedars tomorrow. Saturday's a good day to leave.

Ellen: If they give you an option leave it to the Lord's Day. Yep, the good Lord would . . . .

(Biddy *yawns ostentatiously*.)
You stop yawning. You should read the Bible.

Biddy: Oh Gawd, she's off.

Ellen: There's a lotta wonderful people in the Bible. It's the *greatest* book.

Marian: I feel . . . so light. I feel . . . confident. Just like I used to.

Ellen: Yeh. Yeh, I know, baby. (*pause*) Automation's the big thing but I believe in the Bible.

Biddy: Can't whip up any interest.

Ellen: Just think: Jesus promised paradise to a dying thief in exchange for *one* kind word. Isn't that wonderful?

Biddy: You Yanks . . . so gullible. Mind you . . . the story of the Virgin birth would be very interesting, in my opinion, if you happened to know the people involved personally.

Marian: Ha, ha, ha.

(*Sounds of* Charlie *off stage shouting, 'Good morning, good morning, good morning.' He enters speaking rapidly and takes very short steps. He helps himself to coffee still muttering.*)

Charlie: Good morning good morning good morning good morning good morning good morning good morning. (*sits down right*)

Marian: What energy!

Biddy: You missed breakfast this morning, Charlie.

Charlie: Just finished it. Bloody awful it was, too. Toast burned. Tea stewed. Butter rancid, and I bet this coffee will

155

taste institutional.

Biddy: Ever asked Pythagoras's opinion on the Bible?

Ellen: Pythagoras! That heathen! He's just a bum heathen who believes in the reincarnation racket.

Charlie: (*shouting*) Don't you ladies know my father was a train driver?

Marian: I bet he drove an express.

Charlie: He knew every signal between Euston and Preston. It wasn't all roses, you know. He had to look out for people throwing themselves under the engine.

Ellen: For Chris'sake.

Charlie: Dad ran over 'undreds in his time. Hundreds. Never look back, he used to say, that's the trick, son. Never look back, it only upsets you.

Marian: Never look back.

Ellen: *Never* look back.

Biddy: Never, never.

Charlie: Coming home excited, looking forward to seeing the wife again, the kids, on a windy Autumn afternoon, coming home twenty-four hours early, arms full of things — I dunno — luggage, gifts, flowers . . .

Biddy: Chrysanthemums . . .

Charlie: . . . shutting the front door.

Marian: Too loudly.

Ellen: Using one of your feet because your arms are loaded.

Charlie: An' shouting up the stairs, shouting 'Hullo, there' . . . Nothing. The house empty, the living room empty with a window open.

Marian: That windy Autumn afternoon.

Charlie: And the curtains flying, flying.

　　(Charlie *picks up newspaper. The three ladies look into space. Tannoy comes on.*)

Tannoy: Will Dr Green please report to the superintendent's office? Will Dr Green report to the superintendent's office immediately, please? Thank you.

Ellen: Charlie, you're reading the newspaper upside down.

Charlie: Wha'?

Ellen: Wrong way up — your *Daily Express*.

Charlie: I know what I'm doing.

Ellen: It's upside down.

Charlie: Mind your own business.

Ellen: Why are you reading the newspaper the wrong way round?

Charlie: (*muttering*) Bloody interfering with me. Women!

Ellen: I don't read the newspapers — too much gloom and doom. I've had enough catastrophe in my own life without reading that stuff. My interest in life is me.

Charlie: I always read the *Daily Express* upside down. I know what I'm doing.

Ellen: Biddy, did I tell you how my second husband got decapitated?

Biddy: Yes, an' we know it's all lies.

Charlie: I was enjoying this newspaper. You women mess things up.

Ellen: He worked on a fairground.

Biddy: Lies!

Marian: You've told us, Ellen.

Ellen: My second husband. On one of those machines that take you high up then whirl you round. There was this crane contraption . . . His head got taken off, zoom, clean as a whistle.

(Biddy *cowers in her chair and puts her hands over her ears.* Ellen *goes closer to her, telling* Biddy *who doesn't want to hear.*)

And there he was strapped into the whirling seat minus head. Round and round his body went, just the blood pouring up through his torn neck.

Charlie: *Please,* you trying to make me puke?

Ellen: He was strapped in good. And they didn't stop the music for such a long time.

Marian: (*quietly*) Poor Ellen.

Ellen: Do you want to hear what happened to Hiram, my third husband?

Charlie: No!

Ellen: Okay so he was only a bum window-washer — and he was real slow at it too — but at least Hiram wanted kids which none of my other fellers did. He was only fifty-some but he had no spunk in him. They did a slide of his semen.

Marian: You've told us before, Ellen.

Ellen: Christ, his count was zero. Listen, Marian, I'd have had a different life if I'd had a child. Someone I could cherish. I wouldn't have bin so lonely. You know something? Narcissus

157

didn't drown of self-love. Don't let them give you that stuff, kid. Narcissus drowned because he was so goddam lonely.

Biddy: (*mischievously*) You've got Jesus. How can she be lonely when she's got Jesus?

Ellen: You mocking me? You're so stupid and *you* are mocking *me*. You fat cow. You smell of ostrich's piss.

Biddy: You dung-ridden, poxed . . . .

Ellen: Why you're dirty! You don't clean yourself! If you lay down with the dogs you'd get up with the fleas. Too bad Christ had to die for rats like you.

Charlie: (*shouting*) Ladies, ladies, *please*.

Marian: He's right. You two are always fighting.

Charlie: Can I have some tranquillity, a halcyon moment or two while I peruse this newspaper? Thank you.

(Ellen *giggles*. Charlie *growls, crushes his newspaper, then exits*.)

Ellen: He's attractive when he's masterful. He's a horny little bugger.

(*Pause*.)

Biddy: (*sadly*) It's years, years since I had a man.

(*Lights down*.)

Scene Three

(*The superintendent's office. The door is open. The phone is ringing. Enter* Mr X. *eating crisps. He stares at the phone. He takes a chair, puts it near the desk and stares intently at it as he eats crisps. Enter* Pythagoras. *He sits down in the superintendent's chair. Then he picks up a newspaper and ignores the phone*.)

X: Shall I answer it?

Pythagoras: Better not.

X: It's getting on my nerves.

(Pythagoras *brings his arm over as if bowling at cricket. When his index finger is pointing at the phone it immediately stops ringing.* X *eats crisps unconcernedly*.)

X: You're on form. Bet you could read my thoughts today. Why am I in Dr Aquillus's office?

Pythagoras: Because you want to see Dr Aquillus.

X: (*seriously*) You *are* on form.

Pythagoras: And you're going to complain to him that you feel dead inside like you always do — that your intestines are made of glass.

X: True.

Pythagoras: Sometimes I can only bend a few knives or swords, stop clocks, and instigate a bit of thunder. But today I feel I could raise the dead with an aurora borealis thrown in.

X: You'll be good at the concert tonight.

Pythagoras: When it comes to magic, Exy, things sometimes get out of hand, know what I mean? Once I had a ventriloquist's doll — I'm a pretty good ventriloquist too — but one night — it was at Porthcawl Pavilion — one night, I wasn't saying a word and the damn doll started talking on its own.

X: Sometimes I feel I'm just a puppet.

Pythagoras: I know that feeling.

X: That your words aren't your own? (*pause*) If I had your gifts I'd do so much good in the world. I'd bring down the bullies. Make lightning strike tyrants. I'd make rain fall in India. Stop floods with a secret incantation. Make crooked limbs straight with a touch. Make the old younger and the young happy. That's what I'd do.

(*Enter superintendent, Dr Aquillus.*)

Pythagoras: (*laughing*) No use, Exy, I've tried. Moral profundity is an antidote to magic.

Aquillus: Perhaps God discovered that. Tsk, tsk, neither of you should barge into my office without an appointment. Besides you're Dr Green's patients, not mine.

Pythagoras: I have no confidence in Dr Green. His soul is so polluted.

Aquillus: Soul! What's the soul made of? Phlogiston? Ha, ha, ha.

Pythagoras: Xenophanes mocked me as you do, doctor. I had told him the soul of a man could migrate to a dog. Well, even as I speak now, Xenophanes is tethered to a drainpipe in an empty terraced street and is barking, barking.

Aquillus: Hmm. Dr Green, with his interest in the occult, should be fascinated by all that. But he tells me that apart from your recent medical history, he knows very little about you as you'll only talk about some imaginary life you led in ancient Samos and Croton.

Pythagoras: Green knows nothing about me.

X: (*brightly*) And we know very little about Dr Green.

Aquillus: If you were less taciturn about recent events —

Pythagoras: In Croton I gained more respect by saying little than others did by saying much.

Aquillus: Let us keep to this century. You used to have headaches in thundery weather when you were a small boy. You knew when thunder and lightning would occur.

Pythagoras: Right.

Aquillus: But later you began to think you could control the weather, could bring on thunder with a hey presto.

Pythagoras: That's what Dr Green told you?

Aquillus: At seventeen, you began to think you had extraordinary powers.

X: He has. Pythagoras is a miracle worker. He is in the company of Moses and Jesus.

Pythagoras: Why drag Moses and Jesus into it?

Aquillus: You became interested in following the profession of stage illusionist.

Pythagoras: I was apprenticed. I learnt my trade. Hypnotism. Ventriloquism. And I mastered the fraudulent gadgets. The quickness of the hand that deceives — but that's another thing. More to the point I began to recall more of the way I'd lived in Samos and Croton. And something I can't comprehend would occasionally possess me and I'd become an instrument for it.

X: My bowels are made of glass.

Aquillus: Yes, yes.

X: I feel dead inside.

Aquillus: We'll talk about that later. As a matter of fact I want you to volunteer for the demonstration.

X: No! Definitely not.

Aquillus: Why not?

X: Definitely, definitely, definitely not.

    (Mr X *begins to exit*.)

Aquillus: Don't be alarmed, there's nothing to it.

    (*Exit* Mr X.)

X: (*off*) You're not going to exploit me.

160

Aquillus: (*shaking head*) Like you, he lives in the suburbs of punishment. But you — *you* feel inspired.

Pythagoras: I do see the correspondence of disparate things. That *is* inspiration. I know, too, the secret of irrationality, and I have the gift of approximate, prophetic insight.

Aquillus: Approximate?

Pythagoras: It's like a smell. I can't always be sure. If I told you of my other powers you'd poke fun at me.

Aquillus: No.

Pythagoras: If I told you I have power over animals, over poisonous snakes even, if I told you I could communicate with the souls inhabiting animals — even that parrot there — you'd think I was but a Greek shaman, or more likely that I was deluded and that these claims simply are symptoms of a schizoid personality. You're right. I have such a temperament. So had Isaac Newton, so had Einstein, and indeed they, too, had brief nervous breakdowns.

Aquillus: You don't think that because of your . . . breakdown . . . you imagine that you are Pythagoras?

Pythagoras: No, it is because I'm Pythagoras restored to this discordant century that I've had a breakdown.

Aquillus: Last year you had a partial gastrectomy because of a duodenal ulcer.

Pythagoras: I have a scar to prove it.

Aquillus: That ulcer gave you hell. It punished you. The operation too was a form of punishment.

Pythagoras: So?

Aquillus: Two years ago you admitted to piercing pains in the calves. Three years ago your right lung leaked air. That was painful. You've lived in the suburbs of punishment because you feel guilty.

Pythagoras: Sometimes when I can accurately foretell future events I do feel guilty. I admit that. As if I were a voyeur. As if I looked into a private room where a man is crying and a woman screaming. Of course, sometimes my ability to prophesy has been more ordinary. For instance, I know what horse will win the Derby next week.

Aquillus: (*chuckling*) I gotta horse.

Pythagoras: You're laughing at me again.

Aquillus: I'm sorry. Tell me something more significant. Is your mother alive, Pythagoras?

Pythagoras: Prince Monolulu by one and a half lengths.

Aquillus: Are you married? Tell me that.

Pythagoras: (*eyes closed*) Something in me is out of harmony.

Aquillus: (*loud*) Why won't you tell us anything important about yourself?

Pythagoras: (*opening eyes*) In Samos I had a slave Zalmaxis. I gave him his liberty, and he became a friend.

Aquillus: Oh no, no!

Pythagoras: My father, a Phoenician by birth, was a gem engraver and . . . .

Tannoy: Will Dr Aquillus and Dr Green please come to D Wing immediately? Will Dr Aquillus and Dr Green please proceed to D Wing? Thank you.

Pythagoras: I can't really talk to you. You have no religious intuitions. Don't you know — outside that window is not just a gravel pathway winding between green lawns and high trees. It is revelation. Whichever way you look is revelation.

(*Pause.*)

Aquillus: I'm keeping the students waiting.

(Aquillus *begins to exit.*)

That horse. Prince Monolulu. Is there such a horse?

Pythagoras: Yes.

Aquillus: Ur, hm. What odds?

Pythagoras: (*smiling*) Twenty-five to one.

Aquillus: Mmm. Prince Monolulu.

(*Exit* Dr Aquillus. Pythagoras *bowls as in cricket to point finally at the phone which immediately rings.* Pythagoras *at once picks up receiver.*)

Pythagoras: (*yelling*) Wrong number!

(*He swiftly replaces the phone, then raises his right hand upwards, fingers parted in the mystical position, and straightaway there is a lightning flash followed by a crack of thunder.* Pythagoras *is about to leave when he observes* Dr Aquillus's *white coat which he now tries on.*)

Perhaps I should take over, try to cure them, and form a brotherhood.

(*He is about to take off white coat when* Ken Kennedy, *a young reporter, enters.*)

Kennedy: Dr Aquillus?

162

Pythagoras: (*turning*) Mmm?

Kennedy: I wonder if you could spare me a few minutes?

Pythagoras: I'm not . . . .

Kennedy: Sorry to barge into your office like this. I'm from *The Record*. I just want to give the concert a write-up. I believe my predecessor did so on the last occasion. I hope you don't mind, doctor. I did phone but I got no reply.

Pythagoras: That phone's out of order. Struck by lightning, probably.

Kennedy: Ha, ha, ha, struck by lightning! (*he hands* Pythagoras *his card*) Ken Kennedy. Everybody calls me Ken. I suppose the concert is therapeutic for the patients?

Pythagoras: Or for the doctors.

Kennedy: Ha, ha, for the doctors! I hear there's going to be a poetry reading and madrigals and you have an ex-stage magician.

Pythagoras: Yes, I'm the main . . . I mean Pythagoras, one of our patients, is the main attraction. He's an extraordinary magician and this year we have prevailed upon him to give us a treat. He'll bring down the house, ha, ha, ha.

Kennedy: Pythagoras?

Pythagoras: Yes, a native of Samos who believes in the table of ten opposites, that ten is the sum of the first four numbers, that ten is the most perfect number, that the square on the hypotenuse of a right-angled triangle is equal to the sum of the squares on the other two sides and so forth and so on.

Kennedy: Bloody mad, eh?

Pythagoras: Mr Kennedy, many people say if Jesus came back they'd lock him up in a place like this.

Kennedy: I dare say.

Pythagoras: Anyway, Pythagoras won't be here long. He just has selective amnesia, that's all. He has forgotten certain small things. For instance, he's not absolutely sure whether he is, at present, married.

Kennedy: Small things! Ha, ha, ha. Doctor, you're a card. If he was married, he'd know all right. (*pause*) I've been married four months and four days.

Pythagoras: Theano, oh Theano, dear one.

Kennedy: Wassat?

Pythagoras: Have you heard of the Orphic priesthood?

163

Pythagoras learnt much in Egypt. A very knowledgeable man! Tonight, I'm quite sure he'll astound the audience. I can just picture the end of his act.

Kennedy: How do you mean?

Pythagoras: Pythagoras leaves the stage and still they are clapping. When he returns they clap even louder. The clapping seems as if it will never cease. He is bowing. He takes off one glove, they are clapping. He leaves the stage and they are clapping. The stage is empty and some are standing. The stage is empty and some are leaving. The stage is empty and some are clapping. The stage is empty and few are clapping. The stage is empty and the clapping ceases. The stage is empty and the seats are empty.

    (*Pause.*)

Kennedy: Doctor, that's a very odd description. Anybody could tell you're not an ordinary doctor. One can always tell a psychiatrist.

Pythagoras: You flatter me. All the doctors here agree that Pythagoras is truly a mystery man.

Kennedy: I expect a few certified patients are.

Pythagoras: Mmm. You probably don't appreciate the nature of true magic.

Kennedy: As a doctor, you don't believe in magic, do you doctor?

Pythagoras: The Hippocratic Corpus — though nowadays no doctor may read its seventy books — still informs the spirit of modern medicine in so far as it emphasises the importance of facts and data and the hesitating possibility of generalizing from the particular. Hence if all — shall we say — observed unicorns are white, doctors would assume that unicorns are white invariably, do you follow? They wouldn't be able to recognize a black unicorn as a unicorn.

Kennedy: Unicorns don't exist.

Pythagoras: That's it! You've got the nub of the problem.

Kennedy: I have?

Pythagoras: Yes, very smartly.

Kennedy: Thank you.

Pythagoras: As you would be the first to agree, and as some bright poet has said: 'Unicorns don't exist because they have better things to do!' But the magician has to persuade a unicorn that what it is doing is so very boring that it may as well exist at least for a few seconds.

Kennedy: Ha, ha, ha, doctor you *are* a card, definitely. Yeh, so what you're saying, figuratively speaking, is that this patient Pythagoras can persuade unicorns?

(Pythagoras *closes his eyes, smiles smugly and perceptibly nods.*)

Kennedy: (*mumbling*) Pythagoras. 'Mystery Man Of The Cedars.' (*louder*) Quite a good headline.

Pythagoras: Why not?

Kennedy: 'Searing Truths Of The Insane'. Ye-es, the editor may wear it. I'll get a photographer. Is Pythagoras photogenic?

Pythagoras: Oh, well. (*chuckles modestly*)

Kennedy: I won't be long. I have my bike outside.

Pythagoras: Wait a minute.

Kennedy: Won't be a jiff. Leave it with me, doctor.

(*Exit* Kennedy *in a hurry.*)

Pythagoras: (*calling*) Mr Kennedy, Pythagoras believes in the transmigration of souls and in the beautiful order of things.
things.

(Pythagoras *takes off the white coat, then gazes at the parrot.*)

Pythagoras: Well, what do you think of that, parrot? Speak parrot. The soul of our grandam might haply inhabit a bird.

(*He brings up arms slowly above his head.*)

I said, speak parrot. I, Pythagoras, command you to speak.

(Pythagoras *raises his arms further. His hands above his head touch.*)

Parrot: Thou . . . shalt . . . not . . . eat . . . beans.

(*A great crash of thunder.* Pythagoras *ducks as if to take cover. Lights down.*)

Scene Four

(*The common room.* Ellen, Biddy, Marian.)

Biddy: Christians take their hats off to pray. Jews put them on. Christians put shoes on to visit a church, Moslems at a mosque take them off. Just depends what team you support. May just as well be a follower of Pythagoras.

(*Pause.*)

Ellen: I don't know what the opposite to an orgasm is — but that's what I get when I argue with you.

(*Enter* Charlie *right. Half running, his trousers rolled up above his knees.*)

Charlie: Ladies, ladies, ladies, do you like my legs?

(*Pause.*)

Marian: Hairy.

Charlie: What do you think of them, Ellen?

Ellen: Well, they're all right *individually*.

(*Enter* Mr X *left followed by* Arthur *who stands in the background.*)

X: I'm not going, not going. NOT GOING.

Charlie: What's the matter?

X: He wants me to be the exhibit this morning. It's so demeaning.

Charlie: You're right. It's humiliating.

X: I feel I'm made of glass. I feel . . . feel dead. I am dead — and this is hell.

Biddy: Give me your hand, Mr X.

(Mr X *puts his hands over his face and they all look at each other.*)

Biddy: Exy.

X: Yes.

Biddy: You're always saying you feel dead.

X: I am dead. I've known for years.

Ellen: How do you mean?

X: That time years ago when I was so small.

Ellen: What?

X: When I was small . . . my father came into the room and he just didn't notice me.

Ellen: Aw hell, baby — often my daddy never noticed me either when I was a kid. Yeah, my father was stinkin' drunk mosta the time.

X: Here I am, I called to my father. He looked left at the flowers in a vase, he looked right at the lampshade. Here, here, I said — joyfully — because I thought he was just teasing me, just playing a game.

Marian: And wasn't he?

X: Here, here, Dad. But he walked past me as if I were elsewhere. This way, this way, I said loudly, not knowing now whether to laugh or cry. He looked upward at the crack in the ceiling. He looked downward at the pattern in the carpet.

Biddy: No, no, that way, *that* way.

X: And I thought — what chill pretences, especially when his face turned solemn as if he were about to utter the prayer for the dead.

Marian: Oh, no.

Ellen: Poor kid.

X: But it was when he looked around the room sadly and then knocked off the light closing the door behind him . . . .

Marian: Leaving you in the darkness?

Biddy: Then you *knew*.

X: Yes. And I'm not going to tell all that to . . . *strangers*.

(*Enter* Pythagoras.)

Charlie: Why should any of us be exhibited? We're not guinea pigs. Am I right, Pythagoras?

Pythagoras: Right.

Charlie: Why should we be exploited?

Biddy: Quite right.

Charlie: I have an idea. First, do you all agree the superintendent is an evil dictator like Poly . . . Poly . . . ?

Pythagoras: Polycrates.

Charlie: Exactly. Listen to me, all of you.

(Charlie *climbs on to a chair*.)

Ellen: He's so horny.

Charlie: (*brandishing a water-pistol*) See this revolver? Who's with me?

Marian: That's just a water-pistol.

Ellen: It's not. It's not. I'm with you, bud. We'll kill him.

Biddy: Me too.

Pythagoras: We're all with you.

X: Yes, yes.

Charlie: What about Arthur?

Marian: He hardly says a word except marmite.

Charlie: Get him by the throat and choke an answer outa him.

(Arthur *backs away as they stare at him*.)

Arthur: (*screaming*) Mar-mite.

167

Pythagoras: Leave him alone. He won't give you away. He won't speak. The rest of you. Raise your right hands to swear your allegiance to Charlie.

(Ellen, X *and* Biddy *raise their right hands.*)

All of you. I, Pythagoras command you.

(*First* Marian *then* Arthur *hesitantly raise their hands. There is a great shout followed by cries of 'Speech Charlie', 'Nice one, Charlie', 'Atta boy, Charlie'.* Charlie *swells with pride and pleasure.*)

Charlie: Friends, countrymen, you with question marks in your spines, you with hunches and guesses, betcher a quid, a fiver, every dollar you've got, ten percent, Barclays Bank, National Provincial, Middle and Leg.

Biddy and Ellen: Hear, hear.

Marian: Easy, Charlie. Take it easy, Charlie.

(Charlie *suddenly twists his neck, is suddenly vulnerable and querulous.*)

Charlie: Something won't leave my mind, something like the red beak of a black swan.

(*Hearing this, they all stand quiet but when* Charlie *resumes his speech there are cries of 'Bravo', 'Hear, hear', 'Dead right'. Indeed during the rest of* Charlie's *speech there are cries occasionally from the others of 'Hallelujah', etc. as at a negro spiritual meeting. Even* Marian *joins in finally.*)

Charlie: They twist everything. They put it across *you*, the people. They put *you* in a hospital and call it The Cedars. They put *you* in a slum and call it Sycamore Drive. And what is this so-called Sycamore Drive? One pub, a free house — and a betting shop and a sweet shop and a row of terraced houses with no front gardens, no trees, no sycamores. A bit of a garage maybe and the only colour in the street a bit of an oilpool in the forecourt. And they call *this*, Sycamore Drive. It makes me puke.

All: (*clapping*) Hear, hear.

Charlie: Sycamore Drive, my arse. I went to that Free House and I had to pay for my beer. Went to a local restaurant and ordered Bombay Duck. What did I get? Dried fish.

All: Dried fish.

Charlie: That's what they do. Twist everything. A public school is not for the public. A private in the army has no privacy; a family butcher doesn't butcher the family. Order Toad in the Hole and what do *you*, the people, get?

All: (*shouting*) Quite right. Hear, hear.

Ellen: Isn't he horny? Isn't he just darlin'?

Charlie: I promise you — when I take over, when the superintendent is buried near the thornbush — or the goldfish pool — I promise you, I swear, I swear, — no more demonstrations.

All: Hurrah, hurrah.

Charlie: I promise you no more prying medical students.

All: Hurrah.

Charlie: No more rancid butter, no more stewed tea, no more burnt toast, no more rice pudding, no more school custard. I promise you . . . *dignity*.

All: Hurrah, hurrah.

Charlie: I promise you . . . ev-er-y-thing.

(*Great cheering and hubbub. Enter* Dr Bruce Green *in a white coat. They fall silent raggedly*)

Green: Good morning, Pythagoras. Oh, put that water-pistol away, Charlie. Mr X, come with me, please.

X: Not me.

Green: It's all right. No need to worry.

Biddy: I'll come with you, Exy.

(Biddy *takes his hand and* Dr Green *nods and smiles.*)

Green: That's right. Meanwhile, I think you ought to rehearse the madrigals for tonight. Will you see to that, Charlie?

Charlie: Rely on me, Dr Green.

Green: I'm surprised at you, Marian.

(*Exit* Green *with* X *and* Biddy *right.*)

Pythagoras: I'll change that pistol into a real revolver.

(Pythagoras *then takes a deep breath and shouts a long sentence in a foreign language that sounds like Greek.*)

Charlie: It's all Greek to me. All right, let's 'ave you. First madrigal. By the right one, er two, er three. Move sharp, move sharp.

(*But* Arthur *exits right.* Charlie *half chases after him waving gun but as he does so* Marian *and* Ellen *exit left and he rushes back.*)

Come back, come back.

Pythagoras: Let them go. I'll see to everything.

Charlie: What?

Pythagoras: I'm in charge again.

Charlie: *I* am. Well, I am, aren't I?

> (*Pause.*)

With your permission, of course.

> (*Pause.*)

Have you really changed this into a proper revolver?

Pythagoras: Yes.

Charlie: With bullets in it?

Pythagoras: Of course.

Charlie: And I could kill you?

Pythagoras: Certainly.

Charlie: (*pointing gun*) Aren't you afraid?

Pythagoras: Alas, no. My soul is too impure. Death would mean only another reincarnation, not the final annihilation of self.

Charlie: We could give it a try.

> (Pythagoras *shouts out something dramatic and loud in Greek again.*)

Were those your last words?

Pythagoras: (*shakes head sadly*) Just turned that revolver back into a water pistol, that's all.

> (*As* Charlie *looks at gun, puzzled,* Pythagoras *exits.* Charlie, *putting left finger in left ear and closing his eyes as if expecting a big bang, fires gun into the air. Water comes out. Lights down.*)

Scene Five

(*Lights up. We are inside the lecture theatre of The Cedars. Students are sitting in the first row of the audience and are facing a lectern with a chair each side of it. The medical students are talking amongst themselves but become silent with the entry of* Dr Green *and* Nurse Grey.)

Green: My name is Dr Green. Welcome to those of you who have not visited The Cedars before. I think this morning some of you have come from Westminster Hospital. Anyway, our superintendent will be here shortly with his patients. But before this morning's demonstration may I make a few announcements? Every *other* year at The Cedars we have our *annual* concert, ha, ha. This concert by the patients is to take place tonight at eight p.m. and you are all cordially invited. There will be madrigals and poems. Also one of our patients who, in better times, was a stage magician known as Pythagoras Smith, will also perform.

(*Enter* Dr Aquillus *with* Biddy *and* Mr X. Nurse Grey *directs* Biddy *to a chair left.* X *sits in chair right. Initially* Dr Aquillus *talks quietly to* Dr Green.)

Aquillus: Thank you, Bruce, for holding the fort. Have you told them about the concert?

Green: Yes, indeed. I'm going into London now to see that chap who used to be Pythagoras's agent. I'll be back in good time for the concert.

Aquillus: Good. Fine.

(*Exit* Dr Green.)

Ladies and gentlemen, today I'm going to demonstrate these two patients. Bridget, who is known here affectionately as Biddy . . .

(Biddy *moves her head a little, acknowledging the students.*)

Her obesity is partly due to natural gluttony but partly the result of insulin therapy . . . My second patient calls himself Mr X and has done so since he was cited in a divorce case.

(*The students laugh.* Mr X *does not mind but smiles benignly.*)

Aquillus: Others call him Exy.

X: (*mumbling*) I'm done in.

Aquillus: Mmmm? Do you want to address the students?

X: I'm dead beat.

Aquillus: Speak up, please.

X: I'm dead.

Biddy: (*suddenly rising to her feet*) I should be released. I get depressed sometimes, I even cry sometimes, but that does not make me . . . crazy. I get depressed because I haven't a man here. Frankly, I'm sexually deprived. That's all that's wrong with me. If they released me I might meet a man who excited me, who was interested in me. If I could have a proper relationship with a man I respected my small depression would be over, I assure you.

Aquillus: (*protectively, putting his arm around her*)
Thank you. Thank you for your remarks.

(Biddy *sits down.*)

Aquillus: Well, you must agree that what she says *sounds* reasonable. However, before we return to Biddy . . . .

Student: Can we ask questions, sir?

Aquillus: After the demonstration, certainly. But please let me proceed. Allow me to invite Mr X. to address you. Come forward here, please.

X: Me?

Aquillus: Please. Thank you. I wonder if you would kindly tell these students how you spent your day yesterday?

X: On Thursday?

Aquillus: Yes.

X: I sat in the common room for eight hours.

Aquillus: Er, huh.

X: I drank eleven cups of coffee.

Aquillus: Yes.

X: I stared at the one stain in the ceiling.

Aquillus: Notice the obsessional tone to these comments — *eleven* cups of coffee, *eight* hours in the common room, *one* stain in the ceiling.

X: It looks like Africa upside down.

Aquillus: You stared at the stain that looks like Africa — and afterwards, what?

X: I reclined on the sofa. I put my hands behind my head and spat up at that stain on the ceiling.

Aquillus: Trying to score a bull's eye?

X: Yes. I spat up three times.

Aquillus: *Three* times.

X: Yes. I missed each time.

Biddy: It was raining on Thursday. It was too wet to go out.

X: There was nothing else to do. I counted twelve flies around the electric bulb. I spat up again at the stain three times. Twice, I missed. Then I dozed off. That was Thursday.

Aquillus: And today?

X: Today I'm dead.

Aquillus: Dead, did you say?

Biddy: No, no, no.

(Biddy *has risen from her chair and quickly* Nurse Grey
goes to her and gently settles her back in the chair.)
Aquillus: You're complaining of being dead?
X: Yes. I *am* dead and this is Hell.
Aquillus: I see. Take off your jacket, Mr X.
X: My jacket?
Aquillus: Yes, take it off, please.
     (Mr X *takes his jacket off and puts it behind chair*.)
That's it. Now roll up your right sleeve to show me your
forearm. Nurse Grey, have you a needle?
Nurse: Yes, Dr Aquillus.
Biddy: No, no — don't, don't.
     (Aquillus *takes needle*.)
Aquillus: Tell me, Mr X, do dead men bleed?
X: (*gaily*) Of course not.
Aquillus: And you're dead?
X: Yes.
     (Aquillus *scratches* X's *forearm*.)
Biddy: (*turning away*) I can't stand the sight of blood.
Aquillus: Just a thin trickle. Deal with it, Nurse.
X: That just goes to prove . . .
Aquillus: Yes?
X: That just goes to prove that dead men do bleed.
     (*The students laugh*.)
Aquillus: (*pointing to one of them*) Hoadley — what mental
process have you just seen demonstrated?
Student: Rationalization, sir.
Aquillus: Quite right. An individual committed to a false
premise will rationalize rather than give up his original belief.
Delusion has to be reinforced by apparently logical argument.
Mr X, would you mind sitting down now? Biddy, will you
bring up your chair here, please? Nurse, give Mr X some water.
X: (*smiling happily*) I would like a glass of water.
Biddy: Shall I face them, Dr Aquillus?
Aquillus: Please. Now just tell them about your past — about
what happened to you before you came to The Cedars.
     (Biddy *opens her mouth, closes it again*.)
Go on, dear.
X: They call me X because I'm an ex-person, an ex-human
being. So I'm dead.

(*Again* Biddy *tries to speak but says nothing.*)

Aquillus: She'll begin very soon. We'll just have to be patient.

(Biddy *begins to sob and cry. The students look upset. Then there is a cry of 'Stop it. Stop this demonstration.' It is* Pythagoras *shouting as he enters right.*)

Pythagoras: (*in ringing tones*) Cease.

Aquillus: (*smiling*) Ah, our ex-stage magician. It seems we have a third patient.

Pythagoras: (*to students*) I'm more than a mere magician though I do have psychokinetic powers.

Aquillus: In this sultry June weather Pythagoras sometimes feels he can cause thunder and lightning.

X: Give us some thunder now, Pythagoras.

Pythagoras: When I was a small boy I used to suffer excruciating headaches in thundery weather. I always knew when it was going to thunder and lightning.

X: Please, Pythagoras.

Pythagoras: All right. One summer when I was sixteen I found that if I held the fingers of my left hand in this mystical way, then uplifted my left arm to the sky like this — watch me. One, two, three — I shall count to ten — four, five, six, seven, eight, nine, ten.

(*There is a flash of lightning. The students all talk at once. Then over the hubbub is the sound of thunder.*)

X: (*nodding happily*) Told you so.

Pythagoras:(*looking at his watch*) In five minutes time exactly the nurse there will collapse.

Aquillus: Now, now, that's enough. (*to students*) You're all impressed by that coincidence?

Student: Well, it was uncanny, sir.

Aquillus: The feeling of something being uncanny occurs when what we have hitherto regarded as imaginary appears before us in reality. Uncanny is not quite the right word.

Biddy: When Pythagoras is around things happen.

Pythagoras: (*boasting*) A couple of years ago I visited Sicily and naturally Mount Etna erupted.

Aquillus: Naturally.

Pythagoras: You can be sarcastic. And I can't, of course, be fully understood by these students either. When I say supernatural agencies work through me I know it sounds mad. Yet I am their agent and what happens exceeds human under- standing — like that lightning flash you all witnessed. (*Pause.*) Normally a man in a factory thinks of his domestic problems, is preoccupied. He does not hear the clanging of metal all about him nor the buzz of a bluebottle on a lathe. But if he opened his soul as mine is open then he'd hear everything. He'd hear the harmony of the spheres and he'd see the invisible.

Student: Have you seen a ghost, sir?

Pythagoras: A ghost?

Student: Yes.

Pythagoras: No, I have not seen a ghost.

Student: Ah.

Pythagoras: But I have smelt one.

(*Students laugh*)

Pythagoras: You modern students. You don't realize how privileged you are. In Croton, when I gave my lectures and demonstrations to the kousmatics and neophytes I stood con- cealed behind a curtain. But now, I suppose, you'd like some more thunder?

Students: Yes.

More thunder.

We want thunder.

Pythagoras: Very well. But you know whenever you hear a thunderclap you should all touch the earth as a remembrance of the creation of the universe. (*to Dr Aquillus*) To really believe, people like you must doubt first.

(Pythagoras *again holds his fingers as before and brings his arm higher into the air as he counts.*)

One two three four five six seven eight nine ten.

(*Nothing happens.* Pythagoras *is dismayed.*)

Aquillus: Surprise, surprise, no thunder, no lightning, nothing. Ha, ha, ha — you students all look so disappointed, ha, ha, ha.

Pythagoras: (*shouting*) Stop laughing, Dr Aquillus!

Aquillus: I'm not laughing at you, Pythagoras, ha, ha, ha.

Pythagoras: You idiot quack, you won't be laughing tonight.

Aquillus: Quite right, I'm not laughing, the students aren't laughing.

Pythagoras: Don't patronize me. I promise these students that at the concert tonight I shall make a helluva lightning flash. There will be a thunderbolt. Beforehand I shall offer libations to the gods — offerings of oak leaves to Zeus, laurel to Apollo, rose to Aphrodite, vine to Dionysus. I shall sprinkle lustrations of sea-water from a golden vessel because the sea was the first to come into existence and gold is a most beautiful thing. And at nine o'clock exactly, on the stroke of nine — that number which symbolizes justice and retaliation — the superintendent here of The Cedars will have a coronary and *die*.

(Nurse Grey *now moans slightly and swoons to the ground in a faint. At once* Dr Aquillus *goes over to her.*)

Student: He prophesied she'd collapse.

Aquillus: It's all right, Nurse. You'll be all right. His extravagant talk frightened her, that's all. There, there, she's reviving. Stand back, Biddy.

(Dr Aquillus *is taking her pulse. Everybody seems stupefied except* Pythagoras *who ostentatiously looks at his wrist watch and nods his head triumphantly. Lights down as* Nurse *revives.*)

ACT TWO

Scene One

(*The grounds*. Pythagoras *and* Nurse Grey *are sitting on a park bench*. Pythagoras *has his eyes closed*. Nurse Grey *is reading a paperback*. Arthur *left stage is staring into space. Noise of birds twittering*.)

Arthur: I'll sing.
Nurse: (*still reading book*) In an hour or two when the concert begins.
Arthur: Now.
    (*Pause*.)
Nurse: At the concert. Quite right.
    (*Pause*.)
Arthur: Now.
    (*Pause*.)
Arthur: (*sings*) Oh, Shenandoah, I love your daughter, away you rolling river. Oh, Shenandoah . . . (*he stops*)
Nurse: (*who has looked up to listen*) That was nice. Go on.
Arthur: No.
Nurse: I like that song, Shenandoah.
    (Arthur *stares into space. The* Nurse *reads her book again. A pause*.)
Pythagoras: Nurse, that novel's no good. Let me recommend the last and greatest book in Ovid's *Metamorphoses*.
Arthur: (*sings*) Ye banks and braes o' Bonnie Doon, how can ye bloom sae fresh and fair, how can ye chant ye little bird and I sae weary, fu' of care. Thou'lt break my heart . . . .
Nurse: Don't stop. Why stop?
    (Arthur *stares into space*.)
Pythagoras: Do you think the superintendent a compassionate man, Nurse?

Nurse: Yes, of course I do. Of course he is. He's a fine man. I like Dr Aquillus. A fine, fine man.

Pythagoras: Why?

Nurse: Why? Well, he's kind, you know that. Very punctilious and concerned for you all. He is a model of restraint. Her character is without blemish. She is a wonderful person.

Pythagoras: *She* is?

Nurse: Certainly is.

Pythagoras: The superintendent?

Nurse: Certainly. The way he looks at you . . . candidly. It calms you. He calms the patients. He has a firm but tranquillizing personality. You know he will not let you down. She would never let you down. She's so loyal.

Pythagoras: Who?

Nurse: The superintendent.

    (Arthur, *listening to all this, decides he's had enough and exits quickly singing.*)

Arthur: (*sings*) Oh, Shenandoah, etc.

Nurse: Where are you going?

Arthur: (*off singing*) Away you rolling river.

Nurse: Oh, dear. I forgot to let him have the new tablets.

    (Nurse *exits.*)

Nurse: (*off*) Wait for me, wait for me.

Arthur: (*off, singing*) Oh, Shenandoah, I love your daughter, etc.

Pythagoras: (*chants*) Gold bring me bread, black bring me water, five stones in the air, three on the back of my hand, two in the dust, now you know me, gold bring back our son to us, black bring home our daughter. Red hides the blood, green hides the slaughter, five . . . .

    (*Stops chanting, looks to right and stands up. Enter* Kennedy.)

Kennedy: I've been looking for you everywhere. The editor wasn't keen on my idea. Also the Minister for Education is speaking at the Town Hall at eight thirty and the other reporter — oh well, I can't stay for much of the concert, Dr Aquillus.

Pythagoras: What happened to the photographer?

Kennedy: Drat him.

Pythagoras: What?

Kennedy: Drat him.

Pythagoras: What do you mean, drat him?

Kennedy: Drat him.(*pause*) What's that building?

Pythagoras: D Wing.

Kennedy: (*uneasily*) Is it safe wandering around?

Pythagoras: I'm most disappointed you won't see our great magician at work.

Kennedy: Don't worry, I'll give you all a good write-up. It's peaceful here. Peaceful but lonely.

Pythagoras: Lonely?

Kennedy: Quite. Outside these walls, in the city, it's lonely too. As a reporter I come across — you'd be surprised . . . The other week — you know Marks and Spencer's?

Pythagoras: Uh, huh.

Kennedy: A man was clinging to a ledge on the fifth floor, right up high, threatening to jump off. The ambulance screeched in, the fire engines, the police, a helluva palaver, and hundreds, *thousands*, over an hour or so gathered in the square all looking up at him.

Pythagoras: I can picture it.

Kennedy: He came down on his own at sunset. No more commotion, no problem. Came down meekly. I asked him, mister, I said, why did you climb up there, why did you cause all that trouble, and he said, for the first time in years, he said, everyone seemed concerned about me. Then he took an apple out of his pocket and munched it and the police took him away.

Pythagoras: So?

Kennedy: So I think it's wonderful. There was this man watching the people peering up at him, pointing. Don't you see — he didn't feel on his own any more. He felt all of them willing him not to jump, not to jump. *Don't jump*. So he came down . . . and ate an apple.

Pythagoras: You're a sentimentalist.

Kennedy: No.

Pythagoras: Bet half of them were thinking: jump, you bastard. Jump and be quick about it because I've got to get home, I've got to go to the office, I've got a phone call to make, got a letter to write, so hurry up mate, jump so I can see you beat your brains out on the pavement.

Kennedy: No, no — you've got it wrong. I'm willing to — who's that?

Pythagoras: Mmm?

Kennedy: Now there goes a lonely man. As a reporter you get to know human nature.

(*Enter* Dr Aquillus *who stops to admire some flowers.*)

Pythagoras: That man's dangerous. He has delusions of grandeur. He thinks he's the superintendent, he thinks he's me.

Kennedy: The way he walks you can tell.

Pythagoras: Worse, he attacked another patient last week. He's an animal.

Kennedy: For no reason?

Pythagoras: No reason at all, grabbed him by the throat.

Kennedy: Christ, he looks dangerous. You can see from his face.

Pythagoras: He's most mean too. Stingy.

Aquillus: Hello, there. Taking a breather before the concert?

Pythagoras: Yes indeed.

Aquillus: Excuse me — you're from D Wing?

Kennedy: I'm from the *The Record*. Just came over to have a word with the superintendent about the concert.

Aquillus: Nobody told us.

(Kennedy *is searching in his pockets.*)

Lost something?

Kennedy: Just looking for my cigarettes. I don't seem to have a . . . very sorry I seem to have left . . . Have you a fag, Dr Aquillus?

Aquillus: I don't smoke.

Kennedy: What about you, Dr Aquillus?

Aquillus: I don't smoke.

(*Pause. Sound of a bird whistling.*)

Pythagoras: I used to take the poppy seed and bark of the squill but I've never smoked.

Kennedy: Poppyseeds?

Pythagoras: Oh, ha, ha, ha, that was thousands of years ago.

Aquillus: I use opium sometimes. Yesterday, as a matter of fact.

Kennedy: (*to Pythagoras*) Do you have many drug addicts here?

Aquillus: When I look around me I say, thank God for drugs.

Kennedy: Thank God for drugs?

Aquillus: I don't know what I'd do without them. I do my best, you know. I've not killed too many people over the years.

(*Exit* Pythagoras *to left quickly. At first* Kennedy, *who is staring at* Dr Aquillus *with horror does not notice* Pythagoras's *departure.*)

Kennedy: Where's . . . Hey, come back. What did he slope off like that for?

Aquillus: I really don't know. Er, what was I saying?

Kennedy: You said you hadn't killed too many people.

Aquillus: Ha, ha, ha, no. Well. I presume you want me to talk about our research programme? Or do you want to stick to the concert?

Kennedy: I have to be at the Town Hall before eight-thirty.

Aquillus: Do you know what Machiavelli said?

Kennedy: Mac who?

Aquillus: He said whoever wishes to organize a State and establish its laws must presuppose that all men are mad. I agree. Now periodically men are heaven-sent to guide the destinies of others. I ask myself if I am such a man.

Kennedy: What does Dr Aquillus say?

Aquillus: I say I am — in all modesty.

Kennedy: (*rises*) I think we ought — (*looks at his watch*) I think we ought to join the others.

Aquillus: (*rising*) Damn it all — look at that. People putting the lights on in D Wing and it isn't dark yet.

(*They begin to exit right.*)

Kennedy: What is your opinion of Pythagoras — your magician patient? Is he also an astrologist?

Aquillus: He believes he is the original Pythagoras, you know. Born in Samos at five-thirty.

Kennedy: P.m.?

Aquillus: (*stops walking*) B.C.

Kennedy: Oh, sorry.

Aquillus: The original Pythagoras believed in reincarnation. Our patient believes he can, at times, see into the future. He thinks I'm going to fall down dead with a coronary at nine o'clock tonight, mmm, mmm.

(*They continue to exit right.*)

Kennedy: You ought to tell that to Dr Aquillus.

(*Superintendent grabs* Kennedy *by the arm. Again they stop walking. They stand momentarily extreme right stage.*)

181

Aquillus: You think I ought to tell that to Dr Aquillus?
Kennedy: Yes.
Aquillus: I should tell him of this unpleasant prophecy?
Kennedy: Why, yes.
Aquillus: What did you say your name was?
Kennedy: (*gulping*) Kennedy.
Aquillus: (*gently*) Which . . . one?
Kennedy: Mmm?
Aquillus: Do you like it in D Wing?
Kennedy: I think we should go straight away to Dr Aquillus.
Aquillus: How are you sleeping?
Kennedy: With my wife.

(Aquillus *nods and lets go* Kennedy's *arm. They resume walking and exit.*)
Aquillus: (*off*) My dear boy, are you very depressed? Come to my office and I'll prescribe something.

Scene Two

(*The Common Room.* Biddy, Ellen *and* Pythagoras.)

Pythagoras: I never said that. I believe the physical world is dualistic. Cosmic evil has to exist — otherwise there'd be no perfect harmony.
Ellen: Yeh, yeh, but you suggested Christ wanted to lam outa Jerusalem when they wanted to shaft him.
Biddy: Well, Jesus was causing riots. Jesus claimed he was the Son of God.
Ellen: He *was* the Son of God. I may be a poor, childless, defenceless woman but I *know*.

(*Enter* Mr X.)
Pythagoras: And I'm Pythagoras. You believe Jesus was resurrected but you don't . . . .
Ellen: You're a pagan. Betcher go in for all kinda swinish sacrifices.
Pythagoras: No, I always preached against blood sacrifices. My followers in Croton offered honey and barley on the altars of the gods.

Biddy: There you are. That's very civilized.

Ellen: Look, lover boy, why don't you eat beans? Tell me that, go on.

Pythagoras: You know, I shouldn't divulge the reason for this but I'll tell you. (*pause*) I once carried out an experiment. I put beans in a pot, then buried them in mud. When later I dug them up, the beans had taken the shape of human embryos.

Ellen: Ha, ha, ha, what a load of shit ha, ha,ha, aw go get your hair cut. He's just a punk heathen.

Biddy: An' you're a Jesus freak.

Ellen: Oh, hooey. His religion is so far out you can't argue with him in a rational way.

(*Enter* Charlie.)

X: You should show him more respect. Pythagoras was the first man to recognise the world was a sphere.

Pythagoras: Two and a half thousand years ago — I hate to boast — I was philosopher, mathematician and magician.

Ellen: You shoulda specialized, buster. You won't get anywhere unless you specialize.

Pythagoras: That's what Heraclitus said; 'polymathy' — the learning of many things — 'does not teach understanding otherwise it would have taught Hesiod and Pythagoras, Xenophanes and Hecataeus.'

Ellen: Ain't that what I said?

Pythagoras: Difficult to wear both the white coat of science *and* the magician's purple one. You have to be . . . *very great.* (*pause*).

> White coat and purple coat
> a sleeve from both he sews.
> That white is always stained with blood
> that purple by the rose.

Biddy: Very good. Arthur'd like that.

Pythagoras: And phantom rose and blood most real
> compose a hybrid style,
> white coat and purple coat
> few men can reconcile.

> White coat and purple coat

can each be worn in turn,
but in the white a man will freeze
and in the purple burn.

Biddy: He's better than Arthur.
Charlie: Hm, hm. You think you're a mathematician too, eh?
X: Pythagoras is a mathematical genius.
Charlie: What's eighty-five times sixty-two times sixty-six. Ha, ha, ha. Tell me that, go on. Ha, ha, ha. (*bullying*) I said eighty-five times sixty-two times sixty-six: go on, multiply, multiply, ha,ha,ha,ha,ha,ha.
    (*Pause as* Pythagoras *closes his eyes.*)
(*Pointing*) Mathematician eh? Ha, ha, ha. Ha, ha, ha. Ha, ha, ha.
Pythagoras: (*opening eyes*) Three hundred and forty-seven thousand, eight hundred and twenty.
    (*Pause.*)
Biddy: Ha, ha, ha, ha, ha, ha.
Charlie: Wait a minute. Hang on. Let me write it down. What did you say? I wanna check.
Pythagoras: Three hundred and forty-seven thousand, eight hundred and twenty.
Charlie: Three . . . Four . . . Seven . . . Eight . . . Two..Oh. OK, wait a minute. What did *I* say? What did I ask you to multiply?
Biddy: Eighty-five times sixty-four times sixty-six.
Pythagoras: No. Eighty-five times sixty-two times sixty-six.
Charlie: (*writing*) Eighty-five by sixty-two by sixty-six.
    (Charlie *sits in chair extreme right stage and works out this sum.*)
X: He'll be right. Did you know Cicero visited his tomb at Metapontum?
Ellen: Don't listen to all his stories. He's got the devil in him. Like the parrot in the superintendent's office.
X: Tell them what it was like in the middle of the sixth century, Pythagoras. Tell them what you believe in.
Pythagoras: I believe in the harmony of the opposites, in the transmigration of souls. I believe we should not eat flesh.
Ellen: What a faggot!
Pythagoras: I was interested in mathematics — but

mathematics leads you to ask certain questions about the ultimate nature of reality.

Ellen: Crap.

X: He had disciples.

Pythagoras: I had good pupils. (*pause*) Alcmaeon — he was a good boy. He was the first to dissect animals. He discovered the optic nerve and the Eustachian tubes. An excellent pupil, Alcmaeon. Yes, Croton was a lively place, then. And, later, you know, in Athens, Plato and his boys were much influenced by my teachings. Alas, Plato had a totalitarian sensibility.

Charlie: (*shouting*) He's right, he's right. Three hundred and forty-seven thousand, eight hundred and twenty. Bloody marvel. What a fuckin' mathematician.

X: He never makes errors.

> (*Exit* Charlie *right muttering.*)

Pythagoras: Oh, I do. I did. My style was in the error.

Charlie: (*off*) Fuckin' stupendous!

Pythagoras: I made mistakes, my pupils too. You see, there was a rift eventually. Some were capable of apprehending the scientific side of my teachings but neglected the ethical and magical side. On the other hand there were those who did not eat meat or beans, would not look in the mirror that hangs beside a light, and so on, but forgot the moral purpose of these restrictive rituals, or had no head for science.

Biddy: White coat and purple coat few men can reconcile.

Pythagoras: Exactly. Sometimes, because of my pupils I was misunderstood. They wanted me to be semi-divine. There was so much fabrication and legend-mongering. One idiot babbled I had a golden thigh. No wonder that fool Zeno wrote a book against my teachings, and Heraclitus, the Riddler, that haughty, dark one, criticised me. (*pause*) Now, excuse me, before dinner, I'm going to listen to Bach. I like his mathematical precision. And afterwards I shall let my soul ascend to the heavens in wordless adoration.

Ellen: You'll have to make it snappy, bud, it's nearly dinner time now.

Pythagoras: Don't forget at nine you will all witness the death of . . .

> (*Enter* Nurse Grey *right.*)

. . . of one whom I now realize has the soul of the tyrant.

X: Polycrates?

Nurse: (*cheerfully*) Your daughter's here, Ellen.

Ellen: I have no daughter.

Biddy: What's she brought Dr Aquillus this time? Goldfish? Last time it was that speechless parrot.

Nurse: She's come to hear you sing the madrigals.

Ellen: Gloria?

Nurse: You may have dinner with her in the TV room, if you wish.

(*Enter* Marian *left.*)

Ellen: Gloria's too busy in the pet shop to come and see me.

Biddy: I'd like a puppy. Couldn't she give me a little spaniel puppy?

Nurse: She's waiting for you in the main hall.

Ellen: The devil . . . the devil is in all her animals.

(*Exit* Ellen.)

Nurse: Marian, the superintendent said you can leave next week.

Biddy: (*taking* Marian's *hand*) Oh, Marian, love.

Marian: That's wonderful.

Nurse: Monday, if you like.

Marian: I see Dr Green on Mondays. I'd like one more session with Dr Green.

Nurse: I understand. We'll say Tuesday, shall we?

Marian: That would be good.

(*There is a sound of a bell ringing.*)

Biddy: I'm starving.

(*All except* Pythagoras *begin to exit right.*)

Marian: (*desperate*) Wednesday, Nurse Grey. Wednesday afternoon. Could we leave it till then?

Nurse: (*off*) Of course. Of course, Marian. There's no hurry.

(Pythagoras *is now alone. He turns towards the radio and flings both arms towards it pointing with both index fingers. At once we hear Bach's violin concerto in E. Major. Pythagoras sits down and listens to music with eyes closed. Slow lights down, music slowly fading.*)

Scene Three

(*The superintendent's office.* Kennedy *and* Dr Green *are seated.* Dr Aquillus *is fixing a drink. The door of the parrot's cage is ajar and there is no sign of the parrot.*)

Kennedy: He certainly confused me.

Aquillus: We all make mistakes.

Kennedy: A plausible character, Pythagoras.

Green: He convinced his agent. He really believes Pythagoras Smith is Pythagoras reincarnated. He still, each morning, as once instructed by Pythagoras, keeps his eyes closed and peers at the back of his eyelids. Then he recalls in detail the events of the day before so that he may judge his own conduct and rectify moral error. He's a weird agent.

(Dr Aquillus *has handed a drink to* Kennedy *who stares at it with dismay.*)

Aquillus: Anything amiss?

Green: I think our guest would like a little more than that, Robert.

Aquillus: Oh, of course.

(*But* Dr Aquillus *does not offer any further drink to* Kennedy.)

Apart from his agent you didn't see anybody else?

Green: I called on his former landlady.

Aquillus: Ah.

Green: No use. She's also trying to start a local Pythagorean Society. She herself does not eat beans. Goes about barefoot. Won't walk on the highway. Refuses to pick up anything that's fallen. She didn't think much of me. She said, 'All psychiatrists are mentally wounded.' Maybe she's right.

Aquillus: Rubbish! I think you yourself half believe your patient was born on the Island of Samos in 531 BC.

Kennedy: Ha, ha, ha, ha, ha, ha.

(Kennedy *stops laughing when both doctors look at him unsmilingly.*)

Aquillus: The concert must have started. I think we'd better go.

Green: Last week I gave some sodium amytal to Pythagoras intravenously, talking to him all the time about his childhood while he was in this medicated trance.

Kennedy: Why did you do that?

Aquillus: A psychiatrist has to have the patience of a cat.

Green: To discover things about his early childhood. When he spoke a most strange language I asked our linguist professor patient in D Wing to come over.

Aquillus: Kanellatos? He's too far gone.

Green: No. He told me it was ancient demotic Greek.

Aquillus: You believed him?

Green: He translated several of his remarks. Here they are.

(Dr Green *hands a piece of paper to* Dr Aquillus.)

Aquillus: (*reads*) When I stroked the head of the white eagle it stretched its wings.

Kennedy: I bet, ha, ha, ha.

Aquillus: (*reads*) We must erect a cenotaph for those who break the rules and divulge the secrets of a lifetime . . . Appollonius of Tyana is an imposter. (*looks up*) Who's Appollonius?

Green: No idea.

Aquillus: (*handing paper back to* Dr Green) Well.

Kennedy: It's nonsense.

Aquillus: At best it has a sense of a dream. And I'd say the dream of poor drugged Kanellatos.

Green: I don't think so.

Aquillus: Oh, you Jungians are too credulous. It's a good job our patient cursed me, not you — or else I really do believe that at nine o'clock tonight you would expire. (*to* Kennedy) Please excuse me, I must go to the concert. (*to* Dr Green) I forcefully suggest you join me soon and put that stupid mystical stuff behind you.

(*Exit* Dr Aquillus. Dr Green *fills up* Kennedy's *glass*.)

Green: Allow me. Our superintendent is a great man, but cautious.

Kennedy: I don't think much of him as a psychiatrist, frankly.

Green: Why? He's very astute.

Kennedy: For a kick-off he had difficulty in differentiating the sane from the um — very sane.

Green: We all make mistakes, ha, ha, ha. Cheers!

Kennedy: Cheers!

Green: I made a very clever mistake once. One evening not long after I qualified as a doctor I'd drunk . . . er, my fill, when I was called out to a middle-aged lady. When I was taking her pulse I realized I was a bit tanked up. I couldn't count properly and I said to myself, 'Mmm, a bit too much alcohol.' I must have said it out loud because my patient remarked, very impressed, 'That's very clever of you, doctor.' Ha, ha, ha — she was a *secret* drinker. She thought, ha, ha, ha, that I had caught her out.

Kennedy: Ye — es, but not being able to tell the difference between the sane and insane is, I'd say, a very worrying thing in a psychiatrist.

Green: I don't know. (*pause*) I mean, Dr Aquillus is a very kind man — very kind to me. Keeps me here despite my eccentricities, some of which, even to me, seem almost pathological! Ha, ha, ha, I have many irrational anxieties.

(Dr Green *fills up glasses again.*)

Kennedy: Cheers!

Green: Cheers!

Kennedy: What do you mean by irrational anxieties?

Green: Well, for instance, statistically speaking, there are very few air crashes, agreed?

Kennedy: Agreed.

Green: But do you know, when I'm in a plane about to land or take off, I have a distinct feeling of unease.

Kennedy: Normality gone mad.

Green: What?

Kennedy: Well, Dr Aquillus has his eccentricities too.

Green: Certainly. No question.

Kennedy: For instance, not many people keep an empty cage in their office.

Green: Heavens! The parrot's gone.

(Dr Green *goes over to the cage.*)

Kennedy: Oh. I thought an empty cage was supposed to be symbolic or something.

Green: (*bending*) There are some feathers here. I don't understand.

(Dr Green *rises and soon is peering over the other side of the desk.*)

Kennedy: I've got this Town Hall thing to report at eight-thirty. (*looks at his watch*) Drat.

Green: My God! Come here.

Kennedy: What is it?

(Kennedy *joins* Dr Green. *They stare at something hidden behind the desk.*)

Green: It's beheaded.

Kennedy: That's really sick.

Green: Five months ago somebody beheaded a cat. It was outside my door. We never found out who did it. There was an unsigned note. It said 'Too many mouths to feed.'

Kennedy: Ha, ha, ha, too many mouths, ha, ha, no, no, you're right, it's not funny. All that parrot's blood, uch. That's the trouble with my job. You run into all kinds of unpredictable things. You can't afford to be too sensitive.

Green: That parrot being slaughtered . . .

(Dr Green *pours out drinks.*)

. . . it's very odd.

Kennedy: Yeh, you're always on the outside, know what I mean? More disasters than celebrations. It's a glimpse of a funeral, oh, I dunno, of strangers wearing black, mourning a stranger. 'Parrot shock at The Cedars', yes, I can see that headline.

Green: It's almost like a sacrifice.

(*They both drink from their glasses as lights fade.*)

Scene Four

(*The concert. The curtain is down. In front of it,* Charlie, Ellen, Biddy, Arthur, Mr X *and* Nurse Grey *smile and bow.*)

Nurse: (*stepping forward*) Thank you. Our last madrigal this evening is a most difficult one — but I hope it will amuse you. It is by the fifteenth-century composer, Banchaeri. Ladies and gentlemen, Contrapunto Bestiali.

(*At the end of the madrigal they bow and* Dr Aquillus *enters right applauding. They all exit right to join audience, but* Dr Aquillus *stops* Arthur *and keeps him by his side.*)

Aquillus: Thank you. Most of you know our own bard, Arthur

Haines, who before he made his, er . . . home here had a book of poems published by Faber. It was called, I think, *Marmite and Other Poems.* For some years he's written very little verse. But tonight he agreed to read us a new poem. Please keep your hands in the applauding position for this poem will be short!

(*While* Dr Aquillus *was speaking* Arthur *turned his back to the audience.*)

No, no, no. Good boy. As I was about to . . . .

Arthur: Self.

Aquillus: What?

Arthur: Self. (*yells*) Self . . . by . . . me.

Aquillus: Quite.

Arthur: (*recites*) Elf . . . himself . . . herself . . . thyself . . . myself . . . shelf.

(Arthur *begins to exit left.* Aquillus *chases after him and brings him back stage centre.*)

Aquilus: I must say your skill surprises me. That poem of yours encapsulates most economically not only the spirit of narcissism but the complicated reciprocity between ego-libido and object-libido. Yes, in a logically unassailable way, he differentiates the energy of the ego-instinct from the ego-libido, and the ego-libido from the object-libido. So succinctly, I'm startled. His poem, 'Self', began, you recall, with the word Elf. Elf, no less. A creature that does not exist — any more than do the souls in Dante's *Inferno* or the apparitions in Shakespeare! I do really . . . .

Arthur: (*sings*) Thou'lt break my heart, thou warbling bird, etc.

(*Exit* Arthur *singing left.*)

Aquillus: Oh, well. It is time in any case for the next act. Excuse me. Excuse me.

(*Sound of drums. Curtain rises.* Dr Aquillus *exits left to sit in the audience with students and rest of the cast. In spotlight,* Pythagoras, *right, in top hat and purple cloak and* Marian *wearing the appropriate clothes of a magician's assistant. To the left are three Windsor chairs. On one of them, now in shadow, is a ventriloquist's doll.*)

Pythagoras: My Lord and Lady Mayor, meat-eaters, fish-eaters, all of you who are by murder clothed and by murder fed, pray silence for . . .

Marian: Pythagoras! Magician extraordinary! (*whispers*) Pythagoras, Pythagoras, Pythagoras.

Pythagoras: (*chants*) Gold bring me bread, black bring me water, five stones in the air, three on the back of my hand, two in the dust, now you know me. Gold bring back our son to us, black bring home our daughter.

Marian: (*whispering*) Pythagoras, Pythagoras, Pythagoras, Pythagoras.

(Marian *continues to whisper 'Pythagoras' using sometimes a different tone in her voice, e.g. one of surprise or delight. She is also rhythmically upraising her arms and flapping her hands in a rather comical way.*)

Pythagoras: (*chanting*) Red hides the blood, green hides the slaughter, five knives in the air, three in the back of the hand, two in the dust, now you know me, red bring back our son to us, green bring home our daughter.

Marian: (*whispering*) Pythagoras, Pythagoras, Pythagoras.

Pythagoras: Ha, ha, ha. You like her? I'll put her up for auction.

Marian: (*squeaking*) Pythagoras! (*whispering*) Pythagoras, Pythagoras.

Pythagoras: How much for her beautiful head, how much for her beautiful legs? How much for her red buried heart? C'mon, bid, bid.

Marian: (*whispering*)Pythagoras etc.

Pythagoras: I'll give you a hammer of ebony, nails of silver too, and a varnished plank of pine to hit the nails right through.

(Marian *gives a little scream.*)

So bid, bid, bid. And going, going, gone, says the little pink worm. (*Pause.*)

Now for some thunder.

(Pythagoras *throws both his hands in the air, cries out loudly something long and haunting in Greek. There is a pause. Instead of thunder* Arthur *is heard singing briefly off stage, 'Thou'lt break my heart!'*)

Pythagoras: (*conversationally*) Ladies and gentlemen. The practice of magic is an imprecise art. A bit hit and miss. Sometimes it's chicken but sometimes it's only feathers. Dark, pristine powers have to be coaxed from their arcane hiding places. And when ghosts are the colour of air we must all be supplicants. So please help me. When I say, Gold bring me bread, I want you to repeat that magical phrase. I say Gold bring me bread and you say Gold bring me bread. And so on. You follow? Good. (*loud*) GOLD, BRING ME BREAD.

(*Pause.*)

No, no, no, no, no. Don't be so self-conscious. Are you so over-bred and over-civilized? You're not at home now, you know. No slacking. You can do better than that. You *will* do better than that. (*shouts*) Gold, bring me bread.

Cast, students and audience: Gold, bring me bread.

Pythagoras: Better. But in this free-enterprise society I see you need incentives. If you repeat what I say loud enough, then this beautiful, hypnotized puppet here will remove articles of her clothing, *phrase by phrase. (loud)* Gold, bring me bread.

Cast, students and audience: Gold, bring me bread.

(Marian *removes a bow from her hair.*)

Pythagoras: Black, bring me water.

Cast, students and audience: Black, bring me water.

(*Psychedelic lights on* Marian *as she takes off both her shoes and removes bodice.*)

Pythagoras: Wait a minute. Tease them a bit. What kind of a dame are you? One shoe at a time is enough. Don't rush it. Have you ever seen anyone so keen? Never mind. Now, loud please, loud. FIVE STONES IN THE AIR.

Cast, students and audience: Five stones in the air.

(Marian *removes skirt.*)

Pythagoras: Now, let us see whether you are men or mice. THREE ON THE BACK OF MY HAND.

(*Enter* Charlie *from left running and holding a gun.*)

Charlie: (*shouting*) Off with them, off with them.

(*Exit* Marian *right hastily, chased by* Charlie *who is firing gun.* Pythagoras *raises his hand to call for silence. He addresses the audience.*)

Pythagoras: You all look so disappointed. Let me remind you of the Greek proverb: when you've seen one tit, you've seen two. I recognize that snigger. It's the Archbishop of Canterbury. What? Yes, I do need a new assistant. Now who — pardon? No . . . I don't know where he got hold of a gun.

(*Enter* Biddy.)

Ah, Biddy. Thank you. Sit down down there. Now we have one

chair empty. I need one more volunteer, please. C'mon, c'mon. What about you? Ah . . .

(*Enter* Mr X.)

My old friend, I should have guessed.

X: Shall I sit there, Pythagoras?

Pythagoras: That's right. Biddy, you look sad. Ladies and gentlemen, you don't know the rage that lies behind the face of misery. Biddy, if you smile, I'll make something nice happen. Smile and close your eyes. Splendid. Think of something that you would like to happen *now*. Good. Good. All right, that's simple. For love is simple, am I correct, Exy?

X: Yes.

Pythagoras: Love lasts as long as there are two people, however silent the word.

X: (*rising*) Yes.

Pythagoras: Love is a small flame in a gunpowder factory.

(*X slowly walks towards* Biddy.)

X: Yes.

Pythagoras: Love is like moonlight that makes even a slum beautiful. Love is a woman waiting at a night window,

(*X has taken* Biddy's *hand. She lifts his hand to her cheek, her eyes still closed.*)

who stares down at an empty street of lamp posts. Ha, ha, ha! How sentimental I am. This one too — (*he points at the ventriloquist's doll*) don't you think he also wants to be loved? (*he picks up doll*) Doesn't he look familiar? Ladies and gentlemen, allow me to introduce to you . . .

(*He holds up the dummy to audience. The face of the dummy resembles that of* Dr Aquillus. *Lights all down now except on* Pythagoras *who speaks like a boxing referee.*)

. . . my privilege . . . On my right hand the Champion, DR ROBERT AQUILLUS, SUPERINTENDENT OF THE CEDARS.

Dummy: (*speaking with the taped voice of the superintendent*) I must say your skill surprises me. For you do not exist any more than do the souls in Dante's *Inferno* or the apparitions in Shakespeare. (*pause*) Also let me remind you of your promise. It's nearly nine o'clock, Pythagoras. Do you hear?

(*There is the faint sound of a clock striking.*)

Pythagoras: (*taking a long needle from his cloak*) True, true.

194

Ye-s. Six . . . seven . . . eight . . . NINE.

(*He plunges the needle into doll's left chest from which oozes a red fluid.* Pythagoras *himself makes a very long strange noise before collapsing in slow motion.*)

(*strangulated*) Polycrates.

(Dr Aquillus *rushes on stage followed by* Nurse Grey. *The audience has a quick picture of* Dr Aquillus *listening to* Pythagoras's *chest with a stethoscope while* Nurse Grey *supports his head.* Mr X *and* Biddy *in background watch anxiously. Lights down.*)

Scene Five

(*Superintendent's office, six months later. The parrot's cage has been taken away. Distant sound of carol singers: 'Silent Night.' Outside it is snowing. Soon there is a murmur of voices.* Dr Aquillus *and* Dr Green *are approaching followed by* Charlie.)

Charlie: (*calling off*) Dr Aquillus, Dr Aquillus wait for me. I want to consult you too, Dr Green.

Aquillus: (*off*) Not now, Charlie.

Charlie: (*off*) I told Ellen I'm agin Paul, Peter, The Apostles, The Martyrs, The Confessors, The Evangelists.

Green: (*off*) Charlie!

Charlie: I prefer goddesses to gods.

(*Enter* Dr Green *and* Dr Aquillus *followed by* Charlie *who is holding a bottle of wine.*)

Green: What are you trying to say?

Charlie: I'm trying to say I don't like this place. Especially now, at Christmas. I don't like the company. I want to ask for a transfer.

(*Carol singers stop singing.*)

Green: Where to?

Charlie: (*whining*) I want to be put in the women's ward.

Aquillus: (*looking at wrist watch*) Where's Pythagoras?

Charlie: This is my good-bye present for him.

Aquillus: Where did you get that?

Charlie: I've 'ad it six months. Just before the concert, last

195

summer, Pythagoras told me he could change water into wine. So I got 'old of an empty bottle and I filled it up with a sample.

Green: Sample?

Charlie: Yes . . . a sample.

Green: I don't follow.

Charlie: My own . . . Crikey, you're thick. Dr Green, the doctor-patient relationship is based on the assumption that the doctor has superior knowledge to the patient. Anyway, Pythagoras held it up to the light. Turned the bottle round nine times, uttered some Greek stuff, and lo . . . and *lo* as they say in the Bible. Lo!

Aquillus: You tried some of it?

Charlie: Took a glass. Didn't care for it. Wrong vintage. Would you like a drop yourself, Dr Aquillus?

Aquillus: Oh, no.

Charlie: Don't blame you. It tastes like piss.

(Charlie *makes for door taking bottle with him.*)

Yes . . . say good-bye to Pythagoras for me. (*At the door*) Another thing. It's six months since Ellen decapitated that parrot and you haven't done a bloody thing. (*shouts*) I demand a trial.

(*Exit* Charlie.)

Aquillus: My God, he's getting difficult.

Green: I reduced his dose of chlorpromazine.

Charlie: (*off*) At the Old Bailey. Justice! Justice!

Aquillus: I'm sure Pythagoras won't remember changing that urine into wine.

Green: Ha, ha, ha, wrong vintage.

Aquillus: You know when you finish your paper you should send it to *New Psychiatry*. Pythagoras was such an odd case.

Green: Strange how he improved so quickly after he collapsed at the concert.

Aquillus: The ECT helped.

Green: I hope we aren't being too precipitate, letting him out for Christmas.

Aquillus: I don't think so. In your paper will you cite any parallel cases?

Green: I intend to refer to that woman at Duke University in North Carolina who had telepathic powers.

Aquillus: Mmm?

Green: It so happened she also had thyrotoxicosis. When they operated on her thyroid, curing her, she simultaneously lost her telepathic gifts.

Aquillus: Good heavens. That authentic?

Green: Oh, yes.

(*Enter* Nurse Grey *and* Pythagoras *who looks reduced, ordinary. He is carrying a suitcase.*)

Nurse: Here he is, Dr Aquillus. All neat and shining and ready to say good-bye.

Pythagoras: And to say thank you.

Nurse: (*to* Aquillus) I'll just see if his wife has arrived at the main hall. I'll phone across as soon as I know.

Aquillus: Fine.

(*Exit* Nurse.)

Green: Ready to face the cold, cold snow, Tony?

Pythagoras: Yes.

Aquillus: Best not to go back to stage work. I advise a routine job.

Green: He's taking a temporary clerk's job in the New Year. It's settled.

Aquillus: That should not be too demanding. Yes, that's a good bet — better than my bet ha ha ha on Prince Honolulu last June, remember?

Pythagoras: Monolulu.

Aquillus: Quite right, Monolulu.

Pythagoras: I feel as if I've been absent from my own life.

Aquillus: I understand. You read too much about Pythagoras, thought too much about Pythagoras, dreamed about Pythagoras, asleep and awake. So much so, you, Tony Smith, became . . . ill.

Pythagoras: One thing, doctor, before I go.

Green: Yes.

Pythagoras: Some of the other patients — Biddy, for instance — told me some lines I wrote about a white coat and a purple cloak.

Green: So?

Pythagoras: *I can't write poetry, Dr Green.* And Charlie reckons I did fantastic sums in fifteen seconds flat — *but I'm not particularly good at mathematics.*

Aquillus: Charlie's hardly a reliable witness, Tony. Besides, we all have powers which we do not generally call upon, powers which we hardly know we own. There's nothing preternatural in that.

Pythagoras: I suppose so. Yes, it's absurd, you're right — like thinking, like thinking I could make that phone ring.

(Pythagoras *points at the phone and it rings. The superintendent hesitates, then chuckles and picks up the receiver.*)

Aquillus: Yes. Yes, thank you, Nurse. Tell his wife he's coming over right away.

(Dr Aquillus *puts down phone and laughs heartily.* Dr Green *joins in laughter. But* Pythagoras *puts down suitcase and sits down, evidently disturbed.*)

Aquillus: It was just a coincidence . . . that phone.

Green: Are you all right, Pythagoras?

Aquillus: Don't call him Pythagoras. His name is Tony Smith.

Pythagoras: I'll just sit down a minute. I'll be all right in a sec.

(*The snow outside descends across the window. Very faint now the distant carol can be heard again. Lights gradually down.*)

Curtain

Notes

House of Cowards

p.27 *butties*. South Wales slang, originating in mining, for friends.

pp.29-30 *Saturday Night and Sunday Morning*. The acclaimed first novel by Alan Sillitoe (b.1928). *Doctor Zhivago*, by Boris Pasternak (1890-1960), is a famous novel (later a famous film) about the fate of the intelligentsia in Russia during the Revolution. That George should choose a grittily realistic study of working-class life for his mother and a tragic romantic novel for Miss Chantry, points to important differences between the two women.

p.30 *Botvinnick*. Mikhail Botvinnick, the Russian chess player, was world champion during most of the 1950s.

p.32 *a war going on in Algeria*. A reference to Algeria's bloody struggle with France for independence.

p.33 *Room at the Top*. Laurence Harvey starred in the film of John Braine's best-selling novel of the same title. The theme was the ruthless rise to fortune of a young man in a Northern town. That Hicks has seen this film and regards the hero as a model for his own son is a small gloss on the nature of his fantasies.

p.36 *Victor Sylvester*. A famous bandleader and popularizer of ballroom-dancing.

p.36 *King Shapur*. A king in ancient Persia, as Jay explains. Jay's view of his approach to religious freedom is characteristically overstated.

p.37 *Bertrand Russell*. A famous English philosopher better known in the 1950s as a prominent CND activist and the movement's first president.

p.37 *Colonel Nasser*. Leader of Egypt who nationalised the Suez Canal in 1956.

p.37 *Archbishop Makarios*. Greek Orthodox archbishop and Cypriot national leader who, in the 1950s, led the island's struggle for independence.

p.37 *Nat Lofthouse or Billy Wright or Johnny Haynes*. Famous English international soccer players who were at their peak in the 1950s.

p.37 *by-election at Rochdale*. Ludovic Kennedy, husband of the actress and ballet-dancer Moira Shearer (star of the film, *The Red Shoes*), and later a tv personality, narrowly failed to secure a famous Liberal victory.

p.44 *glass breaking*. The groom crushes a glass underfoot as part of the Jewish marriage ceremony. There are various historical explanations of the act but, here, Abse is using it as symbolic of the breaking of the hymen in the act of sexual intercourse. It dramatizes the strength of Hick's sudden sexual urge. Miss Chantry's reaction, therefore, is suggestive and humorous.

p.50 *a big march this Easter to a place called Aldermarston.* The Campaign for Nuclear Disarmament (CND), launched in 1958, organized a fifty mile mass protest march from London to the Atomic Weapons Research Establishment at Aldermarston, Berkshire. The Aldermarston marches' were huge popular successes and for a time became annual events.

p.53 *Shemtov.* Israel Baal Shem-tov (or Tob) (1700-66) stressed that prayer rather than study of the Holy Books best brought communion with God. He thus gave the generally illiterate masses a sense of spiritual power.

pp.53-4 *Hassidism.* Hassidic Jews observed the highest standards of religious and moral behaviour. Miss Chantry, revealingly, chooses to emphasize the annihilation of the self in ecstatic behaviour.

p.54 *there's nothing so small . . . gold.* Miss Chantry refers to Rainer Maria Rilke, *Poems from the Book of Hours*, trans. Babette Deutsch (London, Vision Press, 1949), p.11. She quotes slightly inaccurately. The lines should read: "There is nothing too small, but my tenderness paints/ it large on a background of gold". That she quotes from the *Book of Hours* indicates the emotional and romantic nature of Miss Chantry's religious feeling. The misquoting may well reveal frustrated desire.

p.56 *Ab. Ben Ruach ACadsh.* This version of 'abracadabra' consists of the first letters of the Hebrew words for Father, Son and Holy Spirit. Traditionally, the phrase was believed to have the power to ward off evil spirits, disease and other misfortune. Here it is a slightly obscure indication of the crowd's spiritual longing and of its unease.

p.69 *Fenner Brockway, Canon Collins, Michael Foot, Frank Cousins.* In 1958, respectively, a Labour MP and famous peace campaigner, a Canon of St Paul's who was Chairman of CND, a well-known left-wing MP (who later became leader of the Labour Party), and a trade-union leader who became a government minister and MP.

p.73 *Kay Francis, or Myrna Loy or Norma Shearer or Loretta Young.* Mrs Hicks's comparisons are all famous Hollywood film stars of the 1930s and 40s.

p.74 *the latchet . . . unloose.* Miss Chantry quotes the words of John the Baptist about Christ (*John*, 1, 27).

p.74 *Zacharias.* Husband of Elizabeth and father of John the Baptist. For doubting Gabriel's announcement that the aged Elizabeth would give birth he was struck dumb until John was born. See *Luke*, 5, 5-25. This allusion, plus her previous quotation (see note above), shows Miss Chantry identifying with John the Baptist, a pointer to how, from a religious point of view, she regards herself.

p.78 *Song of Soloman.* The quotation is from 11, 3.

The Dogs of Pavlov

p.90 *Ambrose, Harry Roy, Henry Hall.* All dance-band leaders in the 1930s.

p.90 *WILSON END VIETNAPALM.* Harold Wilson was Labour Prime Minister during much of the 1960s. 1968 saw massive demonstrations against the Vietnam War and, particularly, against USA tactics, which involved the use of napalm bombs (incendiary devices made from jellied petrol).

pp.96-7 *those lines of Yeats.* From 'The Circus Animals Desertion'.

p. 99 *Charlie Girl . . . Lock Up Your Daughters.* All West End hit plays from the period.

p.105 *Biafra.* The eastern region of Nigeria. Its attempt to secede from the Nigerian Federation in 1967 led to a fierce civil war.

p.105 *Enoch Powell.* Conservative MP once notorious for his opposition to coloured immigration.

p.107 *Farouk.* Playboy King of Egypt deposed by a military coup in 1952.

pp.108-9 *STOP YANKEE BUTCHERS NOW.* A reference, of course, to US involvement in the Vietnam War.

p.116 *Pavlov's dog.* This key reference in the play is to the work of the Russian psychologist, Ivan Pavlov (1849-1936), who used dogs to investigate conditioned reflexes and the relationship between psychological stress and brain function. The play's title, therefore, makes a statement about Daly's attitude towards his subjects.

p.127 *Mine is a most peaceful disposition . . . .* Daly is quoting from Heinrich Heine (1797-1856), *MisBedanken und Einfälle* (Thoughts and Ideas), Section 1. Abse first read the quotation in a footnote to Freud's essay 'Civilisation and its Discontents' (*Complete Psychological Works*, standard edition, ed. James Strachey, London, The Hogarth Press & Institute of Psychological Works, 1961, xxi, 110[n]).

p.128 *James Joyce who took as his slogan Satan's 'Non Serviam': 'I will not serve'.* The reference, strictly, is to *Portrait of the Artist as a Young Man* (1916), in which Stephen Dedalus, in rejecting his faith, repeats "I will not serve", a quotation used in a Jesuit sermon to illustrate Satan's sin of pride.

Pythagoras (Smith)

p.150 *Anaximander*. Greek astronomer (b. 610 BC) who suggested the spherical nature of the Earth and that the entire universe is subject to a single law.

p.152 *Samos*. Greek island in the Aegean sea important as a cultural centre, especially during the sixth century BC. Pythagoras is regarded as the most famous Samian. To him are atrributed a belief in reincarnation, the establishing of principles governing the musical scale, and the famous theorem.

pp.157-8 *Narcissus*. In mythology a beautiful youth who saw his own reflection in water, fell in love with it, pined away, died, and turned into the flower.

p.159 *aurora borealis*. Often spectacular luminous atmospheric effects usually found in the southern hemisphere.

p.159 *Porthcawl pavilion*. Porthcawl is a small seaside resort in south Wales. As Abse told a tv interviewer in 1983, an illusionist called Pythagoras once performed at the Pavilion theatre.

p.159 *Xenophanes*. A sixth century BC iconclastic Greek poet and philosopher.

p.160 *Croton*. Now 'Crotone', a southern Italian city to which Pythagoras emigrated from Samos to escape the tyranny of Polycrates. In Croton he founded a religious society which eventually governed the city. Tyranny (of a kind) and expulsion are important ideas in Abse's play.

p.160 *Prince Monolulu*. A flamboyant racing tipster during the post-World War Two period known for his slogan, "I gotta horse".

p.163 *the table of ten opposites*. These refer to mathematical principles established by Pythagoras and his followers. They reflect the idea of universal harmony which, in the play, is replaced by the 'white coat/ purple coat' oppposition.

p.163 *Theano*. Said to have been Pythagoras's wife.

p.163 *Orphic priesthood*. A religious movement in the encient world based on concepts of the after-life and the need to reconcile the divine and the evil elements in man.

p.181 *Machiavelli*. Sixteenth century Florentine diplomat. His book, *The Prince* (1513) is concerned with what rulers must do to retain power.

p.183 *Heraclitus . . . Hesiod . . . Hecataeus*. Learned Greeks contemporary with Pythagoras. Heraclitus followed Anaximander in suggesting a theory of universal harmony based on the reconciliation of opposites.

p.184 *Cicero*. (106-43 BC), the famous Roman writer and orator. Pythagoras had retired from Croton to Metapontum, following a conspiracy against him, and died there.

p.185 *Zeno.* (335-263 BC), founder of the Stoic school of philosophy. He argued that the only real good is virtue, therefore to possess it is to be happy, regardless of anything that may happen.

p.188 *Appolonius of Tyana.* A Neopythagoran sage at the beginning of the Christian era. He led the life of an ascetic wandering teacher said to possess miraculous powers.

p.188 *Jungians.* Followers of Carl Gustav Jung (1885-1961), founder of Analytical Psychology. Jung argued that through extreme mental states (often dreams) a person could establish the truth about himself through contact with the Collective Unconscious.

p.190 *Banchaeri . . . Contrapunto Bestiali.* Adriano Banchaeri (usually Banchieri) (1568-1634) was an Italian composer of 'Madrigal Comedies', humorous compositions in some of which (such as the one featured in the play) the singers made animal noises. That the patients are allowed to perform this is perhaps revealing of the medical staff's attitude towards them.

A Note on Texts and Further Reading

1. Plays

House of Cowards

First published version of the play is in Dannie Abse: *Three Questor Plays* (Lowestoft: Scorpion Press, 1967). This volume also contains 'Gone' and 'In the Cage', plus a short introduction by Alfred Emmet of The Questors Theatre.

The poem, 'The Meeting' was first published in *Tenants of the House* (London: Hutchinson, 1957). It was reprinted in *Collected Poems 1948-1976* (London: Hutchinson, 1977).

The Dogs of Pavlov

The first published version of this play is *The Dogs of Pavlov* (London: Valentine Mitchell, 1973). This edition includes Abse's essay, 'The Experiment', and Professor Stanley Milgram's two letters. ('The Experiment' is reprinted in Dannie Abse: *Miscellany One* (Bridgend: Poetry Wales Press, 1981.)

For 'The Joker in the Pack' see W.H. Auden, *The Dyer's Hand and Other Essays* (London: Faber & Faber, 1963), pp. 246-72.

Pythagoras (Smith)

Title apart, the present text is unaltered from that published as *Pythagoras* (London: Hutchinson, 1979). That edition includes an introduction by Abse (incorporating his introduction to the broadcast of 'Funland' in 1971) and the poem sequence, 'Funland'.

For 'Mario and the Magician' see Thomas Mann, *Mario and the Magician and Other Stories*, trans. H.T. Lowe-Porter (Harmondsworth: Penguin Books, 1988).

2. Criticism

John Elsom, 'Dannie Abse' in *Contemporary Dramatists*, ed. James Vinson (London & New York: St James Press & St Martin's Press, 1973), pp. 13-16.

Dannie Abse, *A Strong Dose of Myself* (London: Hutchinson, 1983), pp. 81-89.

John Cassidy, 'The Plays of Dannie Abse: Responsibilities', *The Poetry of Dannie Abse*, ed. Joseph Cohen (London: Robson Books, 1983), pp. 85-96.

Tony Curtis, *Dannie Abse*, Writers of Wales Series (Cardiff: University of Wales Press, 1985).

3. Poetry

For Abse's poetry see *White Coat, Purple Coat: Collected Poems 1948-1988* (London: Hutchinson, 1989).